TIME

AND ETERNITY

AN ESSAY IN THE PHILOSOPHY

OF RELIGION   *BY W. T. STACE*

PUBLISHED BY PRINCETON UNIVERSITY

PRESS AT PRINCETON NEW JERSEY, 1952

GREENWOOD PRESS, PUBLISHERS
NEW YORK

PREFACE

THIS BOOK, WHILE IT IS AN ATTEMPT TO SET OUT THE fundamental nature of religion, also seeks to deal with the greatest spiritual problem of the modern world, the conflict between religion and the philosophy of naturalism implicit in science. Commonly the conflict between science and religion has been taken to mean the inconsistency between particular discoveries of science and particular religious dogmas; for instance, between evolution and the "special creation" of man, geology and the first chapters of Genesis, biblical criticism and the inspiration of the Bible. And when it is said, as it often is today, that the battle of science with religion is now over, what is apparently meant is that such discussions as these are now for the most part happily forgotten. But the real conflict, which is not over, never was about these matters. It went, and goes, much deeper. It has to do with the opposition between two antagonistic general views of the world. The first is the vision of the world as a moral and divine order, governed in the end by spiritual forces. The second, which is derived from science, but is not itself a part of any science, is the vision of the world as completely governed by blind natural forces and laws, which are wholly indifferent to moral and spiritual ideals. This conflict which, so far as the modern world is concerned, dates from the time of Newton, is still in full swing. It is very far from happily settled; and it is a complete delusion to suppose that the new physics of the present day throws any light on it. The first great thinker of the modern world to understand its true meaning was Immanuel Kant, whose philosophy was—at least in one of its many aspects—an attempt to find a reconciliation. Kant wasted no time on the superficial aspects of the problem, but went straight to the root of the matter, the problem of the opposing world-views. But after his death, the theologians and anti-theologians fell to squabbling again about miracles and the age of the earth. The present book owes much to Kant, although the solution offered differs from his.

The solution offered is not, of course, novel in the sense that it belongs to no previously known type of religio-philosophical thinking. If it were, it would hardly have much chance of being true. The fundamental thought, which it seeks to work out in perhaps a slightly new way, is that all religious thought and speech are through and through symbolic. And this insight is perhaps as old as religion itself. In our own day it informs the work of Professor Tillich. In earlier days one finds it in Schleiermacher and, I believe, even in that pillar of Catholic orthodoxy, Thomas Aquinas.

Perhaps I ought to say something here about the relation of this book to an article I published in the *Atlantic Monthly* for September 1947 under title "Man against Darkness." For that article was widely attacked as atheistic —although I should prefer to call it an affirmation of naturalism—while the present book is a defense of religion. How, it is asked, is this possible? I am not too deeply concerned to defend my consistency—since it is not a crime to change one's opinion—but as a matter of fact the inconsistency, in so far as any exists, is much less than would appear at first sight. For I do not in this book retract naturalism by a jot or a tittle. On the contrary, I reaffirm it in toto. But I endeavor to add to it that other half of the truth which I now think naturalism misses. How it is possible for naturalism and religion—atheism and theism, if you prefer it—to be but two sides of one truth, is the same as the problem how God can be both being and non-being, as one of the most ancient of religious and mystical insights proclaims that He is, or how He can be both the Eternal Yea and the Eternal Nay, as Boëhme affirmed. And the attempt to resolve this problem, so far as the human mind can do so, is one of the main themes of this book. Therefore I must refer the reader for further explanation of the matter to the body of the book itself.

After Kant, I owe more to Rudolph Otto's *The Idea of the Holy* than to any other book. I have also been influenced by Aurobindo's *The Life Divine.* I owe to Professor Walter Kaufmann the references in Chapter 2 to Jewish mysticism and to Mr. Fadlou Shehadi the references to Islamic mysticism. I owe many other debts, too numerous to list here. A few of them I have acknowledged in the body of the book. Many others, no doubt, will be obvious to the reader.

The quotation from T. S. Eliot's *Four Quartets* in Chapter 5 is by permission of Harcourt, Brace & Company.

W. T. S.

Princeton
November 1951

CONTENTS

CHAPTER 1. WHAT RELIGION IS   3

CHAPTER 2. THE NEGATIVE DIVINE   9

CHAPTER 3. THE INTERPRETATION OF
            THE NEGATIVE DIVINE   28

CHAPTER 4. THE POSITIVE DIVINE   50

CHAPTER 5. TIME AND ETERNITY   69

CHAPTER 6. RELIGIOUS SYMBOLISM   91

CHAPTER 7. TRUTH, REALITY, ILLUSION   116

CHAPTER 8. THE DIVINE CIRCLE   136

CHAPTER 9. MYSTICISM AND LOGIC   153

INDEX   167

CHAPTER 1 WHAT RELIGION IS

"RELIGION," SAYS WHITEHEAD, "IS THE VISION OF SOMETHING which stands beyond, behind, and within, the passing flux of immediate things; something which is real, and yet waiting to be realized; something which is a remote possibility, and yet the greatest of present facts; something which gives meaning to all that passes, and yet eludes apprehension; something whose possession is the final good, and yet is beyond all reach; something which is the ultimate ideal, and the hopeless quest." [1]

These words evidently express a direct intuition of the writer. They well up from his own personal religious experience and therefore stir the depths in us who read. What he says is not a faded copy of what someone else has felt or thought or seen, as the majority of pious utterances are—hackneyed and worn-out clichés, debased by parrot-like repetition, although they too, poor dead things, once issued fresh-minted from a living human soul. Here and there amid the arid hills of human experience are well-springs and fountain-heads of religious intuition. They are the original sources of all religion. They need not always be of great grandeur. They may be humble rivulets of feeling. Or they may give rise to great rivers of refreshment flowing through the centuries. But always, great or small, they bear upon themselves the stamp of their own authenticity. They need no external proof or justification. Indeed they are incapable of any. We know them because the God in us cries out, hearing the voice of the God in the other, answering back. The deep calls to the deep.

Whitehead's words are of this kind.

Note first their paradoxical character. To the "something" of which they speak are attributed opposite characters which barely avoid, if they do avoid, the clash of flat con-

[1] A. N. Whitehead, *Science and the Modern World*, chapter 12.

tradiction. Each clause is a balance of such contradicting predicates. The meaning cannot be less than that paradox and contradiction are of the very essence of that "something" itself.

Note, too, the final words. That something which man seeks as his ultimate ideal is the "hopeless quest." This is not a careless expression, an exaggeration, a loose use of words. It is not rhetoric. If this phrase had come at the beginning of the passage, it might have been toned down in the succeeding sentences. But it strikes the final note. It is the last word.

And one can see why. For religion is the hunger of the soul for the impossible, the unattainable, the inconceivable. This is not something which it merely happens to be, an unfortunate accident or disaster which befalls it in the world. This is its essence, and this is its glory. This is what religion *means*. The religious impulse in men *is* the hunger for the impossible, the unattainable, the inconceivable—or at least for that which is these things in the world of time. And anything which is less than this is not religion—though it may be some very admirable thing such as morality. Let it not be said that this makes religion a foolish thing, fit only for madmen—although indeed from the world's point of view the religious man *is* a madman. For, mad or not, this impulse lies deep down in every human heart. It is of the essence of man, quite as much as is his reason.

Religion seeks the infinite. And the infinite by definition is impossible, unattainable. It is by definition that which can never be reached.

Religion seeks the light. But it is not a light which can be found at any place or time. It is not somewhere. It is the light which is nowhere. It is "the light which never was on sea or land." Never was. Never will be, even in the infinite stretches of future time. The light is non-existent, as the poet himself says. Yet it is the great light which lightens the world. And this, too, the poet implies.

Religion is the desire to break away from being and existence altogether, to get beyond existence into that nothingness where the great light is. It is the desire to be utterly free from the fetters of being. For every being is a fetter. Existence is a fetter. To be is to be tied to what you are. Religion is the hunger for the non-being which yet is.

In music sometimes a man will feel that he comes to the edge of breaking out from the prison bars of existence, breaking out from the universe altogether. There is a sense that the goal is at hand, that the boundary wall of the universe is crumbling and will be breached at the next moment, when the soul will pass out free into the infinite. But the goal is not reached. For it is the unspeakable, the impossible, the inconceivable, the unattainable. There is only the sense of falling backward into time. The goal is only glimpsed, sensed, and then lost.

One thing is better than another thing. Gold is perhaps better than clay, poetry than push-pin. One place is pleasanter than another place. One time is happier than another time. In all being there is a scale of better and worse. But just because of this relativity, no being, no time, no place, satisfies the ultimate hunger. For all beings are infected by the same disease, the disease of existence. If owning a marble leaves your metaphysical and religious thirst unquenched, so will owning all the planets. If living on the earth for three-score years and ten leaves it unsatisfied, neither will living in a fabled Heaven for endless ages satisfy it. For how do you attain your end by making things bigger, or longer, or wider, or thicker, or more this or more that? For they will still be *this* or *that*. And it is being this or that which is the disease of things.

So long as there is light in your life, the light has not yet dawned. There is in your life much darkness—that much you will admit. But you think that though this thing, this place, this time, this experience is dark, yet that thing, that place, that time, that experience is, or will be, bright. But this is the great illusion. You must see that all things, all places, all times, all experiences are equally dark. You must see that all stars are black. Only out of the *total* darkness will the light dawn.

Religion is that hunger which no existence, past, present, or future, no actual existence and no possible existence, in this world or in any other world, on the earth or above the clouds and stars, material or mental or spiritual, can ever satisfy. For whatever is or could be will have the curse on it of thisness or thatness.

This is no new thought. It is only what religious men have always said. To the saint Narada the Supreme Being offered whatsoever boon his heart could imagine—abundance of life, riches, health, pleasure, heroic sons. "That," said Narada "and precisely that is what I desire to be rid of and pass beyond." It is true that the things here spoken of—health, riches, even heroic sons—are what we call worldly, even material, things. But they are symbolic only. They stand for all things of any kind, whether material or non-material—for all things, at least, which could have an existence in the order of time, whether in the time before death or in the time after.

It is true that simple-minded religious men have conceived their goal as a state of continued existence beyond the grave filled with all happy things and experiences. But plainly such happy things and experiences were no more than symbolic, and the happy heavens containing such things have the character of myth. To the human mind, fast fettered by the limits of its poor imagination, they stand for and represent the goal. One cannot conceive the inconceivable. So in place of it one puts whatever one can imagine of delight; wine and houris if one's imagination is limited to these; love, kindness, sweetness of spiritual living if one is of a less materialistic temper. But were these existences and delights, material or spiritual, to be actually found and enjoyed as present, they would be condemned by the saint along with all earthly

"the end o
Godhead."

In simila
darkness,"
waste." ⁵ I
darkness,"
consists in
that God is
medieval m
Dean Inge
nothingness
In Jacob B
as well as "
positive and

Since Go
being nor t
Thus all par
a spiritual r
suggestion t
sion of attril
via negativa
acters of wh
ingness of t
we proceed
Him first all
qualities, an
Him among

In Jewish
finds freque
of Jewish M
is frequently

⁴ *ibid.*, p. 2
⁵ W. R. Ing
⁶ *ibid.*, p. 11
⁷ Rufus Jon
⁸ Scholem, p

joys. For they would have upon them the curse, the darkness, the disease, of all existent things, of all that is this or that. This is why we cannot conceive of any particular pleasure, happiness, joy, which would not *cloy*, which—to be quite frank—would not in the end be boring.

"In the Infinite only is bliss. In the finite there is no bliss" says the ancient Upanishad.² And we are apt to imagine that this is a piece of rhetoric, or at least an exaggeration. For surely it is not strictly speaking true that in the finite there is no happiness at all. No doubt the saint or the moralist is right to speak disparagingly of the mere pleasures of sense. But is there, then, no joy of living? What of the love of man and woman, of parent and child? What of the sweetness of flowers, the blue of the sky, the sunlight? Is it not quite false that there is no bliss in these? And yet they are finite. So we say. But we fail to see that the author of the verse is speaking of something quite different from what we have in mind, namely of that ultimate bliss in God which is the final satisfaction of the religious hunger. And we think that this ultimate blessedness differs only *in degree* from the happy and joyful experiences of our lives. Whereas the truth is that it differs *in kind*. The joys, not only of the earth, but of any conceivable heaven—which we can conceive only as some fortunate and happy prolongation of our lives in time—are not of the same order as that ultimate blessedness. We imagine any joyful, even ecstatic, experience we please. We suppose that the blessedness of salvation is something like this, only more joyful. Perhaps if it were multiplied a million times. . . . But all this is of no avail. Though we pile mountain of earthly joy upon mountain of earthly joy, we reach no nearer to the bliss which is the end. For these things belong to different orders; the one, however great, to the order of time; the other to the order of eternity. Therefore all the temporal joys which we pile upon one another to help our imaginations, are no more

² Chandogya Upanishad.

an in
in Ii
caus
tions
that
deve
that
com
India
fully
ticall
That
plicit
ful n
the u
The
it has
emph
and J
velop
I w
tive c
"God
In an
is, a N
We :
speak
stand
hart (
head,
the la
wilde
the ne

It is incomprehensible, for it cannot be comprehended." [17] The force of this "No, No" is apparent. Whatever attribute you suggest for Brahman, whether it is material or mental, the answer is always, no. And this, as we have seen, is equivalent to the assertion that Brahman is Nothing.

The major tradition of Vedantic India has followed this lead. The great philosopher Sankara, writing in the seventh or eighth century A.D., speaks of the Ultimate as the unqualitied Brahman. But since Hinduism recognizes both the negative and the positive aspects of the divine, since Brahman both "is" and "is not," and since thereby a contradiction is engendered, Sankara seeks to resolve it by postulating two Brahmans. There is the "higher" Brahman, who is qualityless, and the "lower" Brahman, having qualities. The former is wholly impersonal, the latter is the personal God of popular religion. He is Ishwara, the creator of the universe, and to him are ascribed the usual noble qualities, goodness, love, power, activity, righteousness, which are everywhere ascribed in our everyday thinking to the Ultimate. But for Sankara the qualityless Brahman alone is the true Ultimate, the qualitied or lower Brahman being no more than its first manifestation.

This is indeed the great riddle of the religious consciousness—how God can be both Being and Non-Being. And a contradiction can, of course, be solved by the separation of the contradicting predicates. The same thing cannot be both square and circular. But one thing can be square and another circular. And this is the solution which Sankara applies to the Being and the Non-Being of God. The Non-Being is ascribed to the higher Brahman, the Being to the lower Brahman. One may be sure it is the wrong solution, for God is One, alike for Hinduism and for Christianity. And the intuition of the religious mind is that God is both Being

[17] "No, No" is Max Muller's translation. More recent translators usually render it "not this, not that." The meaning is in either case the same.

and Non-Being in one. The solution suggested is that of the rationalizing intellect, anxious to do away with the Mystery of God, and to make religious truth palatable to common sense and logic.

It is highly interesting and instructive to find that Meister Eckhart, of course in complete independence of Sankara, adopts the same solution. He places the two contradicting characters, being and non-being, in two different divine existences, although, following Christian tradition and the doctrine of the Trinity, he realizes that both must be, in spite of their difference, one. He distinguishes between the Godhead and God. It is the Godhead which corresponds to Sankara's higher Brahman, and which Eckhart calls "void," "empty," "the nameless Nothing." To God are attributed the usual characters of love, righteousness, and power. The two are one because he identifies Godhead with the Father, God with the Son, while the process from Godhead to God is the Holy Ghost. But, as with Sankara, it is the void Godhead which is the ultimate ground of the world.[18]

There could not be a more striking witness than this utterly independent agreement of the Christian and the Hindu that the great religions of the world, however different in their detailed doctrines, yet spring from one and the same source, the universal religious consciousness of mankind, the universal impulsion of one and the same mystical vision.

Buddhism presents to our exposition the difficulty that, at least in its earlier forms, which are commonly identified with Hinayana or Southern Buddhism, it is said to be "atheistic"; and therefore, it may seem, it can have no theory at all, positive or negative, of the divine existence. I believe this to be a shallow objection to our view that the negative conception of the divine is found in it. But before pointing to its negative conception I must discuss the objection.

---

[18] An elaborate comparison between Eckhart and Sankara is made in Rudolph Otto's *Mysticism East and West*, and to his account I am much in debt here.

Buddhism is, just as much as Christianity or Hinduism, an interpretation of numinous or mystical experience. And mystical experience is the common possession of mankind. It would perhaps be an exaggeration to say that it is identically the same for all men, that the inner experience of the Buddhist mystic is identically the same as the inner experience of the Christian mystic. For the matter of that, even sense experience, on which physical science is founded, is far from being exactly the same for all men. But it is not an exaggeration to say that mystical experience is everywhere unitary in the same sense as aesthetic experience is everywhere unitary. British, American, German, Indian, Chinese, Japanese art are, of course, very different from one another. Yet they have one root in the basic experience of beauty. The human aesthetic sense, as well as the human religious sense, becomes differentiated through conditions of historical, cultural, and geographical determination. In rare cases the differences may become so great that kinship is barely recognizable. Then the dweller in one land may find the art of another land almost wholly opaque and unintelligible. But these *are* rare cases. And even when they occur, it is possible with a little trouble to break through the barriers, and to find that the unitary human spirit flows between compartmental boundaries after all. Indian music, to give only one example, is very strange to the western ear. But still the westerner can accommodate himself to it. And in the majority of cases there is no such difficulty, even though the cultures, between which understanding is sought, are far apart. Thus Chinese painting, Chinese ceramics, make an immediate appeal to sensitive Europeans and Americans. Chinese and Japanese poetry seems poetical to us too. And, to go less far afield, how could the dramas of Sophocles and Aeschylus mean anything to us if they did not appeal to the same basic aesthetic sense in us as was in the Greeks? And it is a platitude that music is a universal language.

As it is with art, so it is with religion. There is but one religious spirit of man, though we speak of many religions. The different religions have been produced by different environments reacting with the same basic human religious sensitivities. And just as an aesthetically sensitive westerner responds instantly to the appeal of a Chinese painting, so the religiously sensitive westerner responds instantly to the spiritual vision and religious passion of the Upanishads.

Buddhism is in some respects more remote than is Hinduism from the mind which has been fashioned under Christian influences (though it must be admitted that in certain other respects, which I need not detail here, the Hindu mind is more alien to us). The differences between Christianity and Buddhism seem at first insurmountable, like those cases in the world of beauty where the art of one nation seems at first utterly opaque to another nation. And the reason is precisely that Buddhism is said to be, and in a sense is, "atheistic." This seems like a complete barrier. We ask at once how this can be a *religion* at all, though we should not deny that it may be a philosophy. For this reason Toynbee —who with all his broad and deep sympathies has yet in this case failed to understand—classes Hinayana Buddhism as a philosophy and denies it the name of religion, though he admits that Mahayana Buddhism is a religion because it is, in its own way, theistic. But in India it is not thought impossible that atheism may be as profoundly religious as theism, nor is atheism regarded by religious men as in itself unspiritual. This is extremely hard for a westerner to understand. Inheriting a Judeo-Christian culture, he identifies religion with a belief in God, and supposes that, although many widely-held religious beliefs may be inessential and peripheral to religion, this one belief is absolutely essential to it, the minimum which is necessary to make a system of thought religious as distinct from philosophical. He does not see that the essence of religion lies in religious *experience*, and not in any belief at all, and that all so-called religious beliefs or doctrines are merely theories *about* the religious experience.

Rudolph Otto, himself a Christian theologian, has correctly seized this point of view, and thereby shows himself, in this matter at least, more profound than Toynbee. He perceives that early Buddhism is based on mystical experience, and is therefore a religion and not merely a philosophy. The point is that Buddhism is just as much an interpretation of unitary human mystical experience as are Christianity and Hinduism. The theory by which the western world explains that sense of religion, that basic numinous, mystical, or religious impulsion or vision, which is found everywhere in the more evolved members of the human race, is to be found in western theological creeds. The theory by which the Buddhist world explains this same sense of religion, this same basic human numinous, mystical, or religious impulsion and vision, appears in its own peculiar doctrines, which do not include the concept of God. However different the two sets of doctrines appear, they are but two different intellectual theories about the same thing. Here again we may use the analogy of art. For although there are not only many different forms of art, but also many different theories of art and of beauty, different systems of aesthetic philosophy—which contradict each other just as radically as do the different religious creeds—yet art is art, and the sense of beauty is the sense of beauty. And so it is with religions.

There is ample evidence that Buddhism is a branch of genuine religion, founded in the mystical sense of man, and not a mere set of barren intellectual propositions. Says Max Muller: "the final goal of the Yoga or of the Sankhya, nay even of the Vedanta and Buddhism, always defies description. Nirvana . . . is a name and a thought, but nothing can be predicated of it. It is what no eye hath seen, and what hath not entered into the mind of man." The truth is that—

however different the two may appear—the concept of Nirvana is the Buddhist interpretation of what the Christian, in his interpretation, calls God.

Before making this point clear we may refer briefly to the concept of the Void in the later, or Mahayana, Buddhism, I quote from Professor A. B. Keith's *Buddhist Philosophy:* "It follows from the fact that we are not concerned with relative knowledge that any definition of suchness is utterly impossible; to apply to it empirical determination is wholly misleading; to say that it is void is to ascribe to it the character which belongs to the phenomena of this world; to say that it exists is to suggest something individual like ourselves which, however, leads to an eternal existence. It is necessary, then, to content ourselves with silence or to choose the simple term suchness or suchness of being, an idea which in its simple form is known to the Hinayana. Suchness is above existence or non-existence or both or neither. It can, therefore, be most easily expressed by negations like the 'Not so, not so' of the Upanishads, and hence it is natural to treat it as the void. But we must not make the error of thinking this a real definition; the void is as void as anything positive." [19]

There is much that is obscure in this passage. But at least it is evident that the Ultimate is in some sense interpreted as void, empty, nothingness. It corresponds to the negative divine in Christianity and Hinduism, although it may be said that there is nothing "divine" in this suchness.

It may be objected that this nihilistic conclusion of the Mahayana Buddhists is reached by means of a sceptical analysis of the phenomenal world, which reduces it to appearance or illusion, and then declares that neither is there

---

[19] Keith, p. 252. Owing to the obscurity of the passage, I am not sure the phrase "the eternal existence" may not be a misprint for "external existence"—which in the context seems to make slightly better sense. What is clear anyhow is that the Ultimate is a void in some sense or other.

any reality behind the illusion. Thus there is, in this view, no Ultimate at all. There is force in this contention. Undoubtedly the conception of the Void was reached by Mahayana Buddhism in a manner wholly different from that of Eckhart or even the Hindu philosophers. And there is a profound difference between saying "the Ultimate is Nothingness" and "there is no such thing as the Ultimate." The former would be accepted by Eckhart, the latter rejected. The former harmonizes with a definite religious intuition, the latter jars on the religious sense. Yet it cannot be said that the two thoughts are wholly different. That the logician may be able to find no difference at all is not to the point. So much the worse for the logician, the difference being plain enough to the religious sense. Yet extremes meet. The nihilism of the Buddhist is a curiously distorted and eccentric version of the genuine religious intuition. It is a kind of caricature. Yet one cannot doubt that the caricature has been derived, through devious and distorting media, from an original religious impulse, just as the most grotesque gargoyle derives originally from the true vision of a face.

But the conception of the Ultimate as Nothing more truly appears in Buddhism in the belief in Nirvana—and here, for our purposes, it is unnecessary to make any distinction between the Hinayana and the Mahayana. On the whole the Buddhist conception of Nirvana is the opposite number of the conception of God in theistic religions. Not that *intellectually* the two conceptions are the same. As *theories* they have perhaps nothing in common. God is a spirit, objective to the worshipper, at least as symbolically conceived. But Nirvana is a state of the saint, not thus objectified. But although God and Nirvana are thus *conceptually* different, they perform the same function for the religious soul as ultimate goal of religious aspiration, as satisfaction of the craving for "that which no eye hath seen, and which hath not entered into the mind of man." Nirvana has neither theological nor metaphysical significance. The Buddha condemned both theology and metaphysics as having no importance for the religious life. God, on the other hand, is in all theistic systems the metaphysical explanation of the world.

Even more important than the point that God and Nirvana play the same role as satisfaction of religious aspiration is the fact that they both have the same root in mystical experience. They are two different theories about the same thing. They are divergent intellectual interpretations of the same basic non-intellectual experience. The experience *is*. It occurs in the human soul. It is not in itself a rational state or process. But no human mind is capable of receiving an experience of any kind without immediately rationalizing it, weaving upon it intellectual constructions, concepts, and theories. The metaphysical concept of God is the theory woven upon the numinous experience in nearly all religions. The non-theistic concept of Nirvana is the Buddhist interpretation of the same numen.

If we descend to a profounder level of analysis, we find that the identity of God and Nirvana is even more striking. For when we spoke of the concept or theory of Nirvana we used a manner of words which was useful, but not strictly speaking correct. Properly speaking, Nirvana is not a concept or theory *of* the numinous experience. It is simply the name of the numinous experience itself. It is the name for that supreme experience wherein all distinction of subject and object is transcended, wherein the ultimate silence, the ultimate peace, the ultimate blessedness is reached, which may be achieved by living men from time to time in momentary flashes, but which with those who have reached the end of the path will last forever. We can call Nirvana a theory or a concept if we like. But in fact it is not so. The whole point about the Buddha's rejection of metaphysics was that he refused to have any theories, because theories in his view do not help toward salvation. In the India of his time, as indeed in all times since then and in all countries,

our question, how the notion of the negative divine enters into Buddhism by way of its concept of Nirvana. We find that in fact both the negative and the positive divine are parts of it, and that therefore there arises for it, as for all true religions, the problem how the divine can be both Being and Non-Being. This is the source of all the puzzles which westerners have found in the concept of Nirvana, as well as of the question which the Buddha's own disciples put to him, whether the saint exists or does not exist after death. They were asking whether Nirvana is Being or Non-Being, when it is in truth both.

Our question, however, concerns at present only the negative aspect of Nirvana. The answer is found in the fact that Nirvana has the same negative side as has the numinous in any other religion. For it is always, in all religions, ineffable, unutterable, inexpressible in any intellectual concepts. The conceptual intellect fails completely to grasp it. For Eckhart God is "the nameless Nothing." Why nameless? Because, as every logician knows, any name, any word in any language, except a proper name, stands for a concept or a universal. Hence there can be no name where there is no concept. And God is ineffable and nameless because no concept can grasp Him. Neither God nor Nirvana stand for concepts. Both are proper names. It is not a contradiction that Eckhart should use the name God and yet declare Him nameless. For though He has a proper name, there is for Him no name in the sense of a word standing for a concept.

Now that which is nameless is necessarily Nothing. For it can have no predicates, no attributes, no qualities, since if it had, it could be classified and named through its attributes. And that which has no predicates is Nothing. This is true alike of the God of Eckhart, of Brahman, and of Nirvana. I have already quoted the dictum of Max Muller that "Nirvana . . . is a name and a thought, but *nothing can be predicated of it.*" This, then, is the negative divine in Buddhism.

Early western interpreters of Buddhism supposed that Nirvana simply meant the annihilation of the soul after death. The ordinary unregenerate man, when he died, was reincarnated in another body. He was constantly reborn, revolving indefinitely on "the wheel of things." To this miserable round Nirvana put a stop. It ended everything. It simply meant the blank non-existence of the soul after death.

These interpreters of Buddhism were in a sense right. They had seized upon one element, the negative element, in Nirvana, ignoring that it also has its positive content. The positive content is "bliss unspeakable." But how can it be at the same time both nothingness and bliss unspeakable? This is, of course, the great enigma—how the divine can both be and not be. But it is important for us to see that it does not arise for Buddhism alone. It arises for the religious consciousness as such; and therefore, in one form or another, it makes its appearance in Christianity, Judaism, Hinduism, and Buddhism. We saw how it arose for both Sankara and Eckhart; and how both of them tried to answer it in the same way, namely by dividing the divine into two beings, and then placing the negative in one, the positive in the other.

The last of the five world religions to be discussed here is Islam. The Islamic conception of God is deeply anthropomorphic, and the notion of His personality and consciousness belongs rather to the positive than to the negative conception of the divine. Hence it is always the positive rather than the negative conception which is emphasized in Islam, and direct affirmations of the nothingness of God are not as a rule to be found in Sufi literature. But there are many passages in their writings which imply it. The following is an example. "Existence," says Jílí "is of two kinds, Absolute Existence, Pure Being, God as He is in Himself, Unknowable, the dark mist (or cloud). . . . The first stage of the descent of the Absolute towards manifestation is the

stage of the Absolute Unity, free from all attributes or relations, but yet no longer the pure undifferentiated Essence." [20]

In what way the first stage of descent, the Absolute Unity,
differs from the original Essence is not here made clear, since
both are undifferentiated unity. But this does not concern
what I want to point out. Although in accordance with the
general Islamic emphasis on His positive aspect, God is here
described as Absolute Existence and Pure Being rather than
as Nothing or Non-Being, yet the negative conception un-
derlies and influences the passage. In the first place the phrase
"the dark mist" as applied to God has a familiar ring. It
reminds us at once of Tauler's phrase "the divine darkness,"
which is unquestionably a direct expression of the idea of
the negative God. Darkness, as we have seen, is a privative
term signifying negativity. Further, the Absolute is declared
to be "without attributes or relations." But this implies the
negative divine because that which is without attributes or
relations is identical with nothing, as we saw in our discussion of Hindu mysticism.

Another Muslim mystic, ibn al-Arabi, wrote: "It is
necessary that you know Him after this fashion, not by
learning, nor by intellect, nor by understanding, nor by
imagination, nor by sense, nor by the outward eye, nor by
the inward eye, nor by perception. . . . His veil, that is phenomenal existence, is but the concealment of His existence
in his Oneness, without any attribute." [21] Here, too, the
absence of attributes in God as He is in Himself is equivalent
to the negative concept of God. And one could multiply
quotations of such passages indefinitely.

The object of the present chapter has not been to dwell
upon, certainly not to attempt a solution of, that ultimate
mystery of religion—how God can be both being and not-

---

[20] Quoted from Margaret Smith, *Readings from the Mystics of
Islam*, p. 118.
[21] *ibid.*, p. 99.

being. We have not yet come to the consideration of the positive character of the divine, much less to the problem how the positive and the negative can be combined. We were to study for the moment only the aspect of God as Nothing, and to show how actually it enters into all the great historical religions. Our next task, before we turn to the exposition of the positive divine, will be to try to understand somewhat better what is the inner significance of the negative divine, what is the religious intuition at its root, and what its implications are.

CHAPTER 3 THE INTERPRETATION OF
THE NEGATIVE DIVINE

THERE COULD SCARCELY BE A MORE PARADOXICAL STATEMENT, more strange-sounding to the man of simple piety, than "God is Nothing." How can such a sentence come from a religious man, or be supposed to express a definite element of a genuine religious consciousness? What difference is there between saying "God is Nothing" and "There is no God"? Thus we enter on the hard task of trying to discover what this utterance "God is Nothing" means for the religious mind, and how we are to interpret it.

The first suggestion is likely to be that the negative divine is no true element of religion at all. Since it must be admitted that it is found in religion, it can be explained only as a morbid growth, a diseased aberration. It is heresy, a departure from the truth. This is, in effect, the view taken by Dean Inge in his book *Christian Mysticism*, and if it were true we should have no need to interpret the meaning of the doctrine, but might simply dismiss it from our further consideration. I hope the following summary of the Dean's views does no injustice to them. The conception of the negative divine came into Christianity, according to him, from the East. It is the old religion of India. It is not indeed "pure error." "There is a negative side in religion, both in thought and practice. We are first impelled to seek the Infinite by the limitations of the finite which appear to the soul as bonds and prison walls. It is natural first to think of the Infinite as that in which the barriers are done away." [1] Nevertheless, except as in this way a "natural" preparation for receiving the truth, the doctrine is in itself error. Moreover it is associated in practice with that oriental rejection of life and of the world which is the very opposite of the Christian activist ideal of work in the world, of building

[1] *Christian Mysticism*, p. 115.

the kingdom of God on earth. "Nearly all that repels us in medieval religious life—it's 'other-worldliness' and passive hostility to civilization—the emptiness of its ideal life—its disparagement of family life—the respect which it paid to indolent contemplation—springs from this one root." [2] And again "Asiatic mysticism is the natural refuge of men who have lost faith in civilization, but will not give up faith in God." [3] And the Dean may seem to have a strong point when he quotes Tauler as saying "Christ never arrived at the emptiness of which these men talk," [4] although Tauler himself had used of God such a phrase as "the nameless, formless, Nothing."

That the doctrine under discussion had its special home in India, and that Indian thought may have influenced, through indirect channels, the development of Christian mysticism, may be admitted. But as I pointed out in the last chapter, the geographical source of a doctrine and its historical causation have no bearing on the question of its truth. That question has to be decided on its own merits. And though the Hebraic sources of Christianity did not emphasize the negative divine, it is, as I shall show, implicit in the ideas of the mystery and incomprehensibility of God, which are common concepts of the religious consciousness of man. Another fact which must be remembered here is that it is a complete mistake to suppose that the Indian religions, Hinduism and Buddhism, taught *only* the negative divine. They were emphatic in their assertion of the positive divine, as was shown in the last chapter. Dean Inge does not explicitly assert that Indian religion was exclusively negative in its conception of God. But if he had kept before his mind the fact that it is not, his criticism of Indian religion, and consequently of its influence on Christianity, would have been seen to lose much of its force. For it is only when the

[2] *ibid.*, p. 112.
[3] *ibid.*, p. 115.
[4] *ibid.*, p. 114.

negative conception of the divine is asserted by itself, without its positive counterpart, that it is error.

It is true that the negative divine, if taken thus alone, leads to inactivism, pessimism, passive resignation, asceticism, retirement from the world, disparagement of the positive values of life in the world. It is also true that Indian mysticism can be accused of so emphasizing the negative divine that these results in fact ensued. For although all Indian religion contains the idea of the positive divine, the opposite idea was in some cases so heavily underscored that the positive divine tended to be either forgotten or given a place of inferiority in the religious consciousness. This latter mistake was made, for example, by Sankara. For in his thought the negative divine is represented by the unqualitied Brahman, which he calls "higher," while the positive divine is relegated to the position of the "lower" Brahman, which he, in effect, conceives as only a concession to popular religion. It is not to be denied that if God is conceived as *only* Nothing, the results will be disastrous. Indeed it is then impossible to distinguish "God is Nothing" from "There is no God." The actual difference between the two, which is felt at once by a religious consciousness which is at all sensitive, lies in the fact that the thought of God as being to man an utter void and abyss of nothingness carries with it, as a faint penumbra in religious feeling, the suggestion of something beyond, something vast and vague, shadowy and tremendous, too great for human apprehension, lying outside the scope of the finite understanding, so that it becomes to that understanding a mere blankness and blindness. Faintly we feel, though we do not fully understand, that, though through symbolic language, through poetry, through imagery and mystic feeling, we perhaps glimpse God or know Him to be in us and in the world, yet if we try to understand what in Himself He actually is, then there arises before the mind so seeking to penetrate the ultimate mystery a blank, a voidness, a veil of darkness hiding the Ultimate. The suggestion of this hidden beyond, which is the positive being of God, is implicit in the statement "God is Void." But "There is no God" expresses only a pure negation.

The Dean is right, then, and he is wrong. He is right in insisting that the negative divine, if taken as by itself constituting the truth about God, is an error. He is wrong if he means to deny, as he apparently does, that the negative divine is a necessary part or element of the religious consciousness. The evidence taken from the great religions of the world, and sketched in the last chapter, is against him. For even if we ignore Indian, Arab, and Jewish sources, the entire Christian mystic tradition supports the belief that the negative divine is a necessary part of religion. And all this evidence the Dean merely explains away.

Nor can the negative divine as it appears in Indian thought be, as the Dean suggests, the mere mistake of a tired civilization. Indeed this charge is absurd in view of the fact that the unknown authors of the Upanishads, who were in India the originators of the doctrine of the negative divine, came from among the early pioneers of a civilization then young and vigorous—however "tired" it may have become two or three thousand years later—pushing its way, precisely as did the American pioneers, across a new continent to become the founders of a new culture and a new family of nations.

Tauler's remark that "Christ never arrived at the emptiness of which these men talk," might indeed give us pause, even though Tauler himself used language which expressed the doctrine of the negative divine. It is true that we do not find in the recorded sayings of Christ any hint of that conception. But we cannot suppose that the revelation of Christ is complete in the sense that all religious truths are to be found in it, so that we could condemn as untrue any idea or thought which is not so found. We may hold that whatever Jesus said of the religious life is true without holding that whatever he did not say is not true. The Christian church would indeed be in a poor way if the latter view were held. One must conceive that Christ's mission was to teach the positive truths about the loving fatherhood of God which are those most needed by plain men who are neither theologians nor philosophers. For it is the love of God, not the voidness of God, which toiling souls require. The doctrine of the void is, after all, an erudite theological or metaphysical truth. Christ did not come before the un-lettered men and women who gathered round him in the guise of a metaphysician or theologian. If Christ did not teach the negative divine—which none of his hearers would have understood—neither did he teach the Platonic or Aris-totelian metaphysics which nevertheless later became parts of the Christian tradition. And if one cannot condemn the Platonic and Aristotelian elements in Christianity on the ground that Jesus did not expound them, neither can one, on the same ground, condemn the doctrine of God as Non-Being. And Tauler himself must have known this when he spoke of God as the "nameless, formless, Nothing." How he would himself have explained the apparent contradiction between his two statements we cannot of course know. But it seems reasonable to suggest that perhaps his rebuke is to be taken as an expression of disgust with the merely nega-tive religion of those mystics who emphasized only the nothingness of God, who seemed to be able to talk of noth-ing else, and so, by ignoring the positivity of God, did vi-olence to the religious revelation.

One must accept the negative divine, then, as a part of religious truth, though only as a part. And we return to the question what it means.

One thing is at once clear. It is connected with the "in-effable" character of religious revelation. That their vision is ineffable is so common and well-known a claim of the mystics in all ages, countries, and religions, that it is not necessary to document it. We may take it for granted, and proceed at once to investigate its significance.

The nature of the connection between ineffability and voidness or nothingness must first be explained. The ineffable is that for which no words can be found. But why can no words be found? The reason is that words, except for proper names, stand for concepts; and concepts connote predicates or collections of predicates. Thus to say that God is ineffable is to say that no concepts apply to Him, and that He is without qualities. But what is without qualities is nothing. Thus we get the "not this, not that" of the Upanishads. And this implies that any statement of the form "God is x" is false. Whether the statement be "God is green" or "God is love," it is false. We shall see later when we discuss what is implied by the idea of the positive divine, that some predicates are more appropriate to God than others. But we are at present at the standpoint of the negative divine. And from that standpoint all predicates are equally inapplicable. Doubtless from this point of view we have on our hands what seems like an insoluble problem. If it is false that God is love, how can it be also at the same time true that God is love, which truth is affirmed in peremptory terms by the religious revelation? But this is after all only the old mystery, the old enigma, how can God both be and not be, how can He be both the blankness of the void and at the same time the fullness of reality? This question we must postpone. It is certain that the ineffability of God implies the falsity of "God is x," where x is any predicate whatever. This will be just as true if we substitute "existent" for x as if we substitute "green" or "love." The proposition "God exists" will be just as false as the proposition "God is green." It is true that there is a dispute among philosophers whether "existent" is a predicate. This is a technical question which cannot be fully discussed here. But I am inclined to think that although the word "existence" may be used in such a way that it is not a predicate, yet in the sense in which it is commonly used it is one. For to say that a thing exists means ordinarily that it forms part of that single system of interrelated experiences which we call the natural order. If we say that the thing of which we merely dream does not exist, we mean that it is not a part of that system. Therefore to say that something exists is to make an assertion about it which might be denied, as we should deny the assertion that something of which we merely dream exists. In this sense, then, we shall have to say that from the point of view of the negative divine the proposition "God exists" is false, since it applies a predicate, namely existence, to God.

Since it is the ineffability of God which leads to the doctrine of the Void, we must next ask what "ineffable" means.

We may first note that it makes no difference whether we say that it is the experience of the mystic which is ineffable or that it is God Himself who is ineffable. For these are the same thing. The experience is not *of* God. For there is in the experience no subject and no object which can be divided or considered as different things.

We may consider some possible meanings of "ineffable." We may perhaps sometimes speak of almost any deep emotional experience as being ineffable. There are "thoughts which do often lie too deep for tears"—and if too deep for tears, then no doubt too deep for words. Is it in anything like this sense that we say that God is ineffable? This cannot be the case. For to say that certain normal, though deep, emotions or ideas, are ineffable is always an exaggeration. We cannot find the words, but they could be found. Or for some reason of shame or reticence, we do not wish to utter them, but they could be uttered. There *are* words which will express them—so far at least as any words ever truly express what we think or feel. No doubt all words fit only loosely the ideas they are intended to convey. There are nuances of thought, shades of feeling, which our vocabulary is too poor to communicate with accuracy. This is true even of sensuous experience. Thus the majority of possible or actual shades of color have no names. But all this has nothing to do with what we mean when we speak of the ineffability of God. This does not mean merely that God is like a shade of feeling, for which we have no word, merely for the accidental reason that the dictionary contains too few words to have a different name for every possible experience.

There is another possible suggestion as to what "ineffable" means in religion. Because it has more plausibility, this will require a longer discussion. There is a sense in which every experience, even that of our physical senses, is ineffable. This means that it is impossible to communicate the experience by words to a person who has not had it. For instance, everyone who has normal vision knows, or can know, the meaning of the word "red." But a man born blind cannot know its meaning. And if you try to explain to him, by means of words, the nature of your color experience, you will find it impossible to do so. You may then say that the experience is ineffable, meaning simply that only a person who has had it can understand it. It is true that persons like Helen Keller use color words intelligently, and you may say that this shows that they understand them. There is a sense in which this is true. But Miss Keller cannot have the same sort of understanding of a color word which a seeing person has, and this is sufficient to establish the ineffability of color experiences in the sense in which it is here important. Of course the same thing is true of all experiences of any kind, whether physical or non-physical. None of them can be conveyed by words to a person whose own experience is entirely lacking in them.

I think that it is very often believed that mystical experience is ineffable in exactly this sense. It is supposed that ordinary people, who are supposed to be non-mystics, are in the same position as the blind man who has not seen colors. They have never had the mystic experience. And therefore a person who has had it cannot explain it to them, and so calls it ineffable.

I believe that this theory of the nature of mystic ineffability, although it may be very widely held, is false, and that so long as it is held no real understanding of religion is possible. It is, from some points of view, both plausible and attractive. Its attractiveness lies in the fact that it is so easy to understand and believe. It reduces the whole problem to the level of science or even plain common sense. We can all speculate that, even on the physical level, there might be sense organs other than those relating to the physical senses which we now possess, and that if there were, we should have experiences which are to us now wholly unimaginable. Perhaps the sensations of some animals and insects give them experiences which are, for us men who do not possess the same sense-receptors, ineffable. Even those high-pitched notes which a dog can hear, but men cannot, are in the same position. And if there are thus physical sensations which are ineffable, why should there not be experiences which we should tend to call spiritual rather than physical, but which are ineffable in the same sense?

But the very plausibility of this suggestion, its common sense character, its facile reduction of the mystery of God to non-mystery, ought to warn us that there is something wrong with it. The mystery of God, we must say, is not like the mystery of what a dog hears, or the mystery of the taste of an onion to one who has never tasted it. The divine mystery would not cease to be mysterious by reason of some discovery of common sense or science, nor by the opening up of some new sense or channel of information. For the divine mystery is absolute, a mystery in itself, not owing to its external relations with what may be supposed to hide it. What lies behind the screen on the other side of my room is no doubt in one sense a mystery to me at this moment. I have but to remove the screen, to look behind it, and the mystery will disappear. But the divine mystery is inherent in the divine, a part of the nature of God, and can never disappear. And this means that it is still a mystery even to the mystic who has directly experienced it, nay, even to God Himself. That is why it is ineffable. The mystery and the ineffability of God are one and the same thing.

One might as well suppose that the problem of the Trinity could be solved by a more advanced mathematics as that the ineffability of God could be made into a straightforward piece of common sense, could be made rational, effable, non-mysterious, by the opening up of some new channel of information or the removal of some screen or barrier. But is not this, one might ask, just what happens when a man passes into the state of mystic illumination? Does he not then understand the mystery? We must answer that it is not so. It is precisely then that the mystery and ineffability of God are made manifest. The mysteriousness of God may be apparent to us. But the mystic experience comes as an overwhelming sense of that mysteriousness, not as a dissipation of it.

The suggestion which we are discussing has the defect that it destroys the uniqueness of God and the uniqueness of religion. God is then only one among other things, although no doubt more great and noble than they are, and also more difficult to understand. But God is not merely more difficult to understand than other things, in the same way as the differential calculus is more difficult to understand than addition and subtraction. If this were so, one could understand God by becoming cleverer. It is not a matter of degree. The Upanishad says flatly that Brahman "is incomprehensible, for it cannot be comprehended." The creed of St. Athanasius agrees with the Upanishad:

"The Father incomprehensible, the Son incomprehensible, the Holy Ghost incomprehensible. . . .
Yet not three incomprehensibles, but one incomprehensible."

All common sense, scientific, or logical explanations of this, such as that God or the mystic experience could be understood if one had greater intellectual powers, or other channels of information, imply that the incomprehensibility spoken of by the creed is merely an exaggeration. I hold on the contrary that the creed means what it says. That which is incomprehensible cannot be made comprehensible by learning more, by being more intellectually gifted, by discovering new instruments and channels of information. The incomprehensibility of God is an absolute attribute of God. It is the same as the mystery of God—inherent, everlasting, and irremoveable.

Let us suppose, however, that the mystic experience is ineffable in the same sense as a color experience or the taste of an onion is ineffable; and let us see what follows from this. A race of men born blind could have no concept of color, much less any color images. But a race of seeing men forms easily both images and concepts of colors. Nor do they experience any difficulty in inventing names, if there happen to be none, for their color experiences. And if the eyes of the human race were to become, for any reason, suddenly sensitive to ultra-violet rays, there would be no difficulty thereafter in framing images and concepts of that new color experience which, we may suppose, would become accessible to us, although it is unimagineable now. Nor would there be any difficulty in inventing words for the new experiences, or in talking to one another freely about them. Just so, on the view under discussion, though we can have no concept of the mystic experience, the mystics themselves should have no difficulty in framing such concepts, in giving them names, and in talking to one another about them; though it is true that we should no more understand their words than a man born blind can understand our color talk. Concepts are formed by noting the similarities or common characters among experiences of the same sort. And just as for us different instances of redness have the common character of being red, which enables us to construct the concept "red," and give a name to it, so the mystic will note the common characters of his different mystic experiences, construct concepts, and give them names.

Now this is nothing like what actually happens. It is, in fact, the very opposite of what happens. For it is the mystic *himself* who finds his vision ineffable and unutterable. It is he who experiences the difficulty, not we. Nor do we ever find him inventing a new vocabulary of words to express his experiences, even when he is speaking to other mystics. He uses the same language which we use, but says the words do not express his meaning. Then why does he not invent new words, as the man who should acquire a new color sense would? We, of course, should not understand them. But he and his fellow mystics would, and they could use the new language at least in communing with themselves and with one another. But nothing of this sort happens. Why not? There is only one possible answer. It is that the impossibility of framing concepts lies, primarily, not with us, but with the mystic himself. And this can mean only one thing, namely that the nature of the experience is such that it is in itself incapable of being conceptualized. To put the same thing in another way, it cannot be apprehended by any kind of conceptualizing intellect, but only by some radically different faculty of the mind. The nature of God is such that it cannot be enmeshed in concepts at all. If it is true that ordinary men do not have the mystic experience—and I think that in any absolute sense this is not true, but that all men have it in some degree—it is not this lack of experience which makes it incomprehensible to us. The fault does not lie with the lack of experience, but with the nature of our intellects. The discursive, discriminating, conceptual intellect cannot apprehend the divine. It cannot be understood by any process of analysis, separation, or re-synthesis by concepts.

This is the meaning of "ineffable," and it is also the meaning of the mystery and the incomprehensibility of God. To comprehend means to understand by means of concepts. And that which is inherently incapable of being apprehended by concepts is inherently incomprehensible. It is for the same reason a mystery. I said earlier that God is a mystery even to Himself. If this seemed a hard saying, it should seem so no longer. It means that God's mind does not move or operate by means of concepts.

It is also clear why the mystic experience must be of this unconceptualizable kind. Intellectual understanding must have some material to work on. Some raw experience must be fed into the meshes of its machinery. Now this implies the separation of subject and object. The intellect is the subject and what is fed into it is its object. Thus it is of the very nature of intellect to involve the subject-object opposition. But in the mystic experience this opposition is transcended. Therefore the intellect is incapable of understanding it. Therefore it is incomprehensible, ineffable.

The same lesson is taught by the insistence of the religious consciousness on the oneness of God. This is not only of Greek or oriental origin. It is not only the One of Plotinus or the One of the Upanishads. It appears with an even greater insistence, as also with a greater sense of mystery, in the doctrine of the Trinity. God, although three, is yet an undivided unity. This oneness of God is not like the oneness of a triangle or a tripod. The tripod, too, is doubtless three in one. But the one in the tripod is divisible into three. And each of the three stands in relation to the other two and to the whole. But the oneness of God is indivisible and relationless. Now this relationless indivisible unity is precisely the character of the mystic intuition as described by all mystics. It is not only the separation of subject from object which is transcended, but all separation. To say this is only to say that the mystic experience is beyond the capacity of the intellect to handle, since it is the very nature of the intellect to operate by means of separation, discrimination, and analysis.

But if God is not to be grasped by the conceptual intellect, how is He to be known or apprehended? The word most commonly used for the mystical apprehension of the divine is "intuition." The word "intuition" is, no doubt, open to abuse. It tends to be vague and ambiguous. Worse than this, people can claim, and do claim, that any absurd idea, which they cherish and cannot rationally justify, is an intuition. But a thing does not in itself become objectionable because it is capable of being abused. We must try to avoid the abuses, but not discard the thing which is abused. And since the word intuition is commonly used of mystical experience, I shall continue to use it.

There is no sense in asking *what* intuition is, any more than there would be sense in asking what the intellect is. Intellect is the name given to the process of understanding objects by means of concepts. Intuition is the name given to the apprehension of the divine in mystical experience. It is conceptless, and without the division into subject and object which is characteristic of the intellect. You can say that you do not believe in intuition, if you like. But in that case you are only saying that you do not believe there is such a thing as the mystic experience, or that it does not have the characters which those who experience it say it has. The point is that, in saying that the mystic experience is intuition, we are not saying anything new about it which renders it liable to any suspicion which did not attach to it before. We are only providing it with a convenient label.

We are now in a position to interpret the meaning of the negative divine. It is no different from the assertions that God is mysterious and incomprehensible. And this is why I said on an earlier page that the negative divine is a necessary element in the complete religious consciousness, for a sense of the ultimate mysteriousness of the world is surely a common element in any basically religious view of the universe. And the negative divine means that God is incapable of being apprehended by concepts. Thus to the intellect He is blank, void, nothing. You cannot attach any predicate to Him, even the predicate "existence," because every predicate stands for a concept, so that to affirm a predicate of Him is to pretend that He is apprehensible by the conceptual intellect. It does not mean that He is not apprehensible at all. For He is apprehensible in intuition.

But here we may fall into another error. In our understandable desire to make sense of religion, to make it comprehensible—in spite of the warning of the Athanasian creed—to make peace between religion and the scientific intelligence, between the mystic and the logician—we try to arrange a compromise. God, we say, is not really unintelligible, He is only unintelligible *to us*. It is only the *human* mind which cannot understand the Ultimate, because it is puny, because it is finite. Incomprehensibility is not therefore, as we asserted above, an absolute attribute of God as He is in Himself; it is relative to our minds only.

The common statement that the finite mind of man cannot understand the infinite is undoubtedly in some sense true, but it is very vague and unclear. To examine it with a view to understanding what it means will throw light on our present problems. The first essential is to understand what are the meanings of the words "finite" and "infinite" here. For this is by no means obvious. We understand in what sense these words are applied to space, time, or a series of numbers. But in what sense could it be said that a mind, any mind, is either finite or infinite?

Perhaps the first suggestion which occurs to us is that the human mind is called finite because of its ignorance, its lack of knowledge. And this must mean that a mind is finite, if it does not know all the facts of the universe. But if so, we must presumably mean by an infinite mind one which does know all the facts. This is open to several objections. In the first place, it is not clear how such a mind would be thereby infinite, unless it is maintained that the universe contains an infinite number of facts. But whether the universe does or does not contain an infinite number of facts is, perhaps, unknown. The most recent scientific speculations suggest a universe finite in space-time, containing a finite number of ultimate particles. And a mind which knew all the facts of such a universe would be, presumably, finite.

Of course, it is always possible to hold that the word infinite, as applied to God, does not really mean what it says. It is merely a pious exaggeration, an honorific term. It just means "extremely large" as compared with a human mind. But this suggestion jars on, and contradicts, our deepest religious intuitions, which insist that God is absolutely absolute, truly infinite, utterly infinite.

This objection, which is based upon the question of the number of facts in the universe, may well be thought formalistic. Indeed we somehow sense that it is irrelevant, that this dispute about how many facts there are to be known is religiously barren; that it is not what we are talking about when we speak of the infinity of God. This is a true intuition. But what it shows is that knowing an infinite number of facts cannot be what we mean by the infinity of the divine mind. And from this follows the important conclusion that in speaking of man's mind as finite we are not referring to the poverty of its knowledge of facts; we are not referring to its ignorance at all. We have been following a false trail.

Evidently, in contrasting the divine and the human mind as infinite and finite respectively, we are not referring to a difference of degree but to a difference of kind. The essential structure of the human mind is different from the essential structure of the divine mind, and it is the structure of our minds which makes them finite and incapable of comprehending the infinity of God. A difference in amount of knowledge would be only a difference of degree. If this were the interpretation, then theoretically a human mind might, by coming to know more and more facts, by coming to know all the facts, become infinite. The point is that there is nothing in the nature of our minds, as such, which could prevent us from knowing all the facts. We are prevented only by two accidental circumstances, first that there is not time because we die too soon, and second that our sense-organs give us access to only a very small range of information about the circumambient universe. Information reaches us only through the five pipes which we call our physical senses. This latter, moreover, is not a defect of the mind at all. It is a defect of our senses. As far as our mental apparatus is concerned, there is no reason to suppose that, if our senses provided us with all the information possible about the world, and if we had the time, we should not be capable of conceptualizing the whole universe, that is, of understanding it. But it is evident that an interpretation which implies that the finiteness of the human mind is only an accidental fact about it, which could conceivably be removed, whereupon it would become as infinite as the mind of God, does not do justice to our religious intuition of the utter nothingness of man before God, and might even be regarded as blasphemous.

It is evidently the structure of our minds, that is, the fact that they operate by means of concepts, which makes them incapable of grasping God, and it must be this also which we mean when we call them finite. The infinity of God cannot be rendered intelligible by concepts. Neither can any other of the characters ascribed to God. This is obvious, for example, in regard to His triune nature. This, which is of His essence, cannot be apprehended by any concept whatever. To suggest that it could be rendered intelligible— which means logical and not self-contradictory—by conceptual thinking, is to suggest that if only we were cleverer than we are we could, while retaining the same mental structure, understand it. It is to suggest that some super-mathematician, some super-Einstein, could succeed in doing this. And this is certainly contrary to the very meaning of the doctrine. And although the doctrine itself cannot be understood conceptually, a good conceptual reason can be given for this fact. For although the Threeness of God might perhaps be grasped by concepts, since it involves division and relations, the Oneness of God cannot. No concept, not even a concept in the mind of God, could understand that Oneness, because it is indivisible and absolutely without relation, whereas the concept as such involves division and relation. For to conceptualize *is* to divide and relate. The concept involves as its basis the relation of similarity between one thing and another thing. God, we must assert, does in His own self-consciousness apprehend His own Oneness. But it cannot be by any concept. It can be only by intuition. In God's self-knowledge there cannot be that separation of subject and object, that separation of this thing from that thing, which is the ineradicable mark of conceptual apprehension. At least His self-knowledge cannot be less than that knowing by being, that identity of subject and object, of this and that, of manyness and oneness, which is called intuition. Indeed this is what God's Oneness means.

Not only is it true of the divine mind that it can know itself only in intuition, but it is true of the human mind also that it can know God only in intuition. Intuition means the same as mystical experience. Nevertheless we are not saying that only the so-called mystics can know God, and that other men cannot. The great mystics are only those in whom the religious sense is exceptionally developed, just as the great artists are only those in whom the aesthetic sense, common to all men, is exceptionally developed. If we hold, as we must, that all men can know God, this is because we must also hold that mystic intuition exists in all men, developed in greater or less degree. And this is evidenced by the fact that the minds of quite common men answer back to the call of the great mystic, just as they answer back to the call of the great poet. If all men were not mystics, as well as poets, then the words of the mystic would be for other men mere nonsense-locutions, senseless concatenations of meaningless noises. But this is not so.

That we can know God only in mystical intuition, and not by the conceptual intellect, may seem to make nonsense of theology. For theology consists of propositions about God. That is to say, it attaches predicates, and applies concepts, to God. The problem thus raised, and the nature of theological truth, will have to be discussed on a later page. For the present we can only say that, as will be generally admitted, religion is not theology. And when it is said that no knowledge of God is possible except in intuition, the knowledge of God which is spoken of is that inner sense of God "within the heart" which is the religious experience, which is in fact religion. A man may know theology without knowing God. And he may know God without knowing theology. And there could not be any theology unless there were first that mystic inner sense. Theology is but the attempt to interpret that experience to the intellect.

But we have not yet learned what is the meaning of saying that the finite mind of man cannot understand the infinite. We have only learned that it does not mean that the infinite could be understood only by some vast, superhuman, perhaps even infinite prolongation of the conceptual intellect. We must try to understand what is meant by calling the human mind finite. In what sense is it finite? And we cannot answer this question unless we first know what could be meant by an infinite mind. An infinite mind does not mean a mind which knows all the facts of the universe, nor is the human mind called finite because it does not know all the facts.

The only rational suggestion is that what makes our intellects finite is that they are suited only to the understanding of finite things, and that they cannot apprehend the infinite. And what cuts them off from the infinite is the fact that they operate by means of concepts. It is only by intuition that the infinite can be apprehended. But why is this? Why cannot the infinite be apprehended by concepts? To see this we must understand that the word "infinite," in the religious sense, has nothing at all to do with that sense of the word in which it is applied to space, time, and the number series. We may call this latter the mathematical infinite to distinguish it from the religious infinite. And it is the confusion between these two which misled us into the false trail of supposing that the infinity of God's mind refers to the amount of His knowledge and that the finitude of man's mind refers to his ignorance.

The religious infinite, or in other words the infinity of God, means *that than which there is no other*. In this sense neither space nor time could be infinite, since space is an "other" to time, and time is an "other" to space.[5] The religious infinite is that which is spoken of by Spinoza in the words "that the conception of which does not need the conception of any other thing from which it must be formed."[6] It is also that which is spoken of by the Upanishads as "the One without a second." And again the Chandogya Upanishad speaks of it in the following way. "Where one sees nothing else, hears nothing else, understands nothing else, that is the infinite. Where one sees something else, hears something else, understands something else, that is the finite."

It may be said that, since the infinite can be thus explained in these conceptual terms, we have thereby understood it by means of concepts. But this is true only in the same sense as it would be true to say that by speaking of the Trinity as "three in One" we have conceptually understood it. And this is not true because the Oneness of the Trinity is without internal relation and without division into Three. Exactly the

[5] This statement is in no way affected by the so-called disappearance of space and time as separate existences in the space-time continuum of relativity physics.

[6] The words quoted are from Spinoza's definition of Substance which is, for him, the infinite.

same is true of the infinite. Since there is to it no other, it might be interpreted as meaning simply the whole universe, the sum of all finite things. But even if the sum of things be infinite in the mathematical sense, it is still infected with finitude because it is a mere collection of finites. And to call this God is merely to use the word God as a new label for what was previously called the universe, and to identify God with the world of finite existences. It is evident that the infinity of God is no more than another name for His Oneness. And this Oneness is not the idea of the mathematical unit. It is the idea that neither within God nor outside Him is there any otherness, any division, any relation—for though we speak of the relation of God to the world, this, as we shall see, is a metaphor. But that which is without otherness, division, or relation—that is to say, the infinite—cannot be apprehended by the concept because the very nature of the concept is to work through otherness, division, and relation. It can be apprehended only in religious intuition.

We can now understand the meaning of the assertion that the finite mind of man cannot understand the infinite God. It does not mean that man cannot know God, for he does so in his religious experience which is intuitive. If this were not so, religious revelation would be impossible. The "finite mind of man" means the concept-generating intellect. It is finite because it cannot grasp the infinite, and it cannot grasp the infinite because it is conceptual. It follows that by an "infinite" mind we do not mean a conceptual intellect which knows everything, and which is an enlargement *ad infinitum* of ordinary conceptual thinking. We mean an intuitive mind.

It also follows that it is not merely *our* minds which cannot understand God, nor is it merely *our* concepts which cannot reach Him. No mind could understand His Mystery —so long as we mean by a mind a conceptual intellect— and no concepts could apprehend Him. And this is the same as saying that He is, in His very nature, unconceptualizable, that His Mystery and incomprehensibility are absolute attributes of Him.

This, then, is the final interpretation of the negative divine. It does not mean that God is unqualifiedly nothing. The meaning of it is that God is nothing *to the conceptual intellect*. It does not mean that He has no positive being, but only that His positive being, though revealed to intuition, is hidden from intellect.

CHAPTER 4 THE POSITIVE DIVINE

IF THE MEANING OF THE NEGATIVE DIVINE IS THAT NO PREDI-
cates are attributable to God, the meaning of the positive
divine is that the religious consciousness nevertheless attributes predicates to Him. And to state these predicates is to
state the positive nature of God. The most general characterization of the negative divine is that God is Non-Being. The
most general characterization of the positive divine is that
God is Being.

What further predicates, beyond mere being or existence,
does the positive conception of His nature apply to Him?
There is ample material in the traditions of the different
world-religions for answering this question. God is, first of
all, a spirit, a mind, a person. This means that He is conceived after the likeness of the human mind. He is mind, not
matter; a psychological being, not a physical being. As a
mind, He is all-knowing, all-wise, all-powerful. He is love,
pity, peace. He is both merciful and just. He can be wrath-
ful too, even jealous. His most outstanding positive characteristic in Christianity is love, in Islam power, in Judaism
righteousness, in Hinduism bliss. These outstanding traits
may be used in the different religious mythologies as basis
for the explanation of His reason for creating a world. Thus
in some Christian writers God created the world as an object for His love. In Hinduism the world is the expression
of God's bliss. Human joy overflows into the body as danc-
ing. Therefore the world is the dance of Siva. "History and
its ruins, the explosions of suns, are flashes from the tireless
swinging sequence of the gestures" [1] of the dance.

We need spend no further time on detailed statements of
the many different positive characters attributed to the Ultimate by the various different branches of the human re-

[1] H. Zimmer, *Myths and Symbols in Indian Art and Civilization*,
p. 155.

ligious consciousness. Much more could, of course, be said.
The point for us is simply that, in spite of the conception
of the negative divine, there *are* such positive characteriza-
tions. For all these words—spirit, mind, person, righteousness, truth, beauty, knowledge, power, love, pity, peace,
blessedness—are the names of attributes or qualities. As such
they are, or imply, concepts. And the problem which we
have to discuss is: How can any concepts, however exalted
the qualities which they represent, apply to that God who,
as we have just seen, is above all concepts whatever? How
can predicates attach to the predicateless? And this is
the same as the problem: how can Non-Being be also Being?

The general answer is that none of these predicates, nor
any others we choose to mention, apply to God in their literal
meaning; they are all symbolical. It is not literally true that
God is a mind, if that word is used in its proper sense as a
stream of psychological events, ideas, sensations, concepts,
emotions, succeeding one another in time. It is not literally
true that God is love, if by love we mean the human emotion which comes and goes and which is the opposite of hate.
The same is true of any of the other terms we use of God.
Not one of them gives us any literal truth. Yet in some way
this symbolic language evokes in us some glimpse, some hint,
seen dimly through the mists and fogs which envelop us,
of that being who stands above all human thought and conception. Moreover it is somehow true that, though all these
words are false, if taken in a literal sense, yet one may be
more false than another. Doubtless it is, strictly speaking,
false to say either that God is love or that He is hate; either
that He is mind or that He is matter. And yet it is truer to
say that He is love than that He is hate, that He is mind
than that He is matter. Indeed we feel that to say that God
is hate would be a hateful falsehood. The negative divine
expresses the fact that all the words we use of God are false.
The positive divine expresses the fact that, in spite of this,

the words we use, if appropriate words are chosen, evoke in us some intuition of the divine nature.

But although the conception of religious language as symbolic is thus seen to be a right approach to our problem, it must not be supposed that it is at once thereby solved. For this only leads us, as we shall see, into further problems. What, we must ask, is the nature of religious symbolism? And how is any truth conveyed by it?

We will approach these questions indirectly. Every doctrine of theology may be understood literally or symbolically. For many years now the trend of more enlightened theological thinking has been away from the literal toward the symbolical. To a large extent this trend has resulted from the pressure exerted by science. A religious doctrine, such as the creation of the world in six days a few thousand years ago, or the special creation of man as a being unrelated to, and undescended from, the lower animal creation, is shown by geology or biology to be false. But the religious consciousness easily accommodates itself to these attacks. It retreats from the literal to the allegorical or symbolic interpretation of its doctrine. In this way more and more of the dogmas of religion gradually pass over from the literal to the symbolical.

But here a crucial question obtrudes itself. How far is this trend toward symbolical interpretation to go, and at what point is it to be stopped? On this question theologians disagree. Fundamentalism is the view that symbolical interpretation should be disallowed altogether as dangerous. All theological doctrines are to be taken literally. This view has at least the merit of being self-consistent. So-called "liberal" theology is characterized by the fact that it admits symbolical interpretation, and the more it allows the more "liberal" it is. But for it the problem arises how far it is to go, where it is to pull up, and on what principle it is to draw the line between what it will regard as symbolic and what it will insist on as literal truth.

In regard to this latter question the usual procedure is to try to distinguish those doctrines which are "essential" to religion from those which are not. The former must be retained as literal, the latter may be given over to the area of allegory. But on what principle does one distinguish the essential from the inessential? To this question there is, so far as I know, no answer. Hence it results that in practice the theologian hangs grimly onto whatever he can as literal, and hands over a doctrine to symbolic interpretation only when the pressure upon him becomes so great that he can no longer hold his ground.

For instance, it is fairly readily agreed that the story of the creation and fall, as given in Genesis, is not literally true. It is an allegory having a deeper religious or moral significance—though there are great differences of opinion as to what this deeper significance is. Again, no one can suppose that God is the father of all men in the literal sense of the word father. But the inner meaning in this case is fairly easy to see. It is that God created man and loves him as a human father loves his children. No doubt, too, God cannot literally be angry or jealous. Anger and jealousy are human emotions which we attribute to God in a symbolic way. Should we stop here? Or should we go on to say that God is not literally a spirit, a mind, a person, that He is not literally righteous, just, merciful, loving, but that these too are merely symbols? This, perhaps we may feel, is going too far. The love of God, at least, is surely "essential." Is it not the very essence of the Christian message to the world? Yet on what principle do we decide this? If one human emotion is to be denied of God, because it is human and because it involves time and change of psychological state in the mind which feels it, how can we consistently attribute to God another such human emotion? And if interpreting God's love symbolically is going too far, what should we say if symbolic interpretation were pushed to its furthest possible point, and it were to be alleged that even to attribute "existence" to

God is a mere symbol? Should we not feel that under this treatment God and religion had evaporated altogether?

In the process of the symbolic interpretation of religious doctrine we can of course stop arbitrarily at any point we please, taking what we want as literal, and allowing the rest to be symbolical. And this is, I think, what many theologians do. But the mind cries aloud for some principle upon which such a decision can be made, and by which it can be justified. This question is, in fact, crucial for religion. A distinguished Christian pastor confided to me that he did not believe the doctrine of the virgin birth to be a literal truth, but added "I believe there is truth in poetry too." [2] I inquired how far he would carry this process of interpreting Christian dogmas as poetry, which doctrines he considered literally true and which as only "poetically true," and how he would distinguish between them. In particular I inquired whether the existence of God is to be considered a literal or a poetic truth. I received no intelligible answer.

But if the symbolistic view of religion appears to be thus dangerous, because it tends to evaporate religion entirely into myth, the literalistic view, it must now be pointed out, is still more dangerous. In fact, it is disastrous. It is the breeding place of scepticism and atheism. They are indeed its necessary outcome. Insist that your dogma is a literal truth, and sooner or later it will be proved to you that it cannot be so. The devil laughs with joy when he finds that the saint takes his beliefs to be *facts*, because he knows that he has then an easy prey. He can show that they are *not* facts. Literalism always lays itself open to successful attack. It is always on this level of literalism that the battle between religion and scepticism takes place. This is the chosen ground of the sceptic, and his strategy will always be to keep on this ground where he knows that in the end he must win.

[2] The word "poetry"—which in this context is apt to suggest the merely imaginary, and therefore by association, the false—was perhaps an unfortunate slip. By poetical he meant symbolical.

Remove the battle to the ground of symbolical interpretation, and the sceptic is without a weapon.

Scepticism always thus attacks the religious dogma in its literal interpretation, but it is nevertheless of two kinds which proceed in two different ways. Either it shows that the dogmas contradict known facts or laws of nature; or it shows that, regardless of any question of fact, the dogmas are internally illogical or self-contradictory. The former kind of scepticism comes usually from science, or at least from a scientifically oriented mind. The latter kind comes usually from philosophy. The former kind tries to show that the dogma contradicts the laws of nature, the latter kind that it contradicts the laws of logic. And it is philosophical scepticism which—though it is less popularly known or understood—is by far the more deadly of the two. The reason for this is that although, as we have seen, no clear distinction can be drawn between what beliefs are essential to religion and what are inessential, the scientific kind of scepticism usually attacks only those doctrines which most people can bring themselves, without any great difficulty, to regard as inessential, while philosophic scepticism attacks those beliefs, such as the existence of God and His goodness, which almost everyone regards as vital.

Very little need here be said of scientific scepticism. Typical of religious beliefs which have come under attack from science are the doctrines of the special creation of man, the literal truth of the Bible as regards history, biology, astronomy, and the like, and also belief in miracles. Religion has easily accommodated itself to science in regard to such matters by adopting allegorical interpretations. It is commonly said that the conflict between science and religion is over, and this may be true, although it is still possible that we ought to be prepared for discoveries from the new young sciences of psychology and sociology which may be difficult to digest.

But the philosophic type of scepticism is quite another

matter, both because it is in itself more deadly and because it cannot be said in any sense that its battle with religion is over. It will repay us to watch the philosophic sceptic at work a little. Consider the following pasage from David Hume:

"Epicurus' old questions are still unanswered. Is He willing to prevent evil, but not able? Then he is impotent. Is He able, but not willing? Then he is malevolent. Is he both able and willing? Whence, then, is evil?" [3]

In considering this passage we should notice that its entire force depends on all the words in it being taken literally. Deity must be thought of as a mind like a man's. "Willing" and "able" must mean exactly what they mean for men. Taken so, we have to say that Hume was right. The charge has never been answered, and never will be. The simultaneous attribution of all-power and all-goodness to the Creator of the whole world is logically incompatible with the existence of evil and pain in the world, for which reason the conception of a finite God, who is not all-powerful, who does His best for the good of things according to His limited ability, has become popular in some quarters. All attempts to show that God's omnipotence, combined with perfect goodness, are compatible with pain and evil—although they fill countless erudite volumes—are patent frauds. One of the commonest has been the assertion that evil is "negative" in nature, mere privation of goodness, and that in consequence it is not a real existence. And God, it is then said, cannot be responsible for a mere absence, and cannot be said to have created what in fact does not exist, nor even to be responsible for "allowing" it to be brought into the world by some other being such as man. A student to whom this view was being explained once asked whether a ship-owner who sent a ship to sea with a hole in its bottom, with consequent disaster to the ship and its passengers, could evade responsibility by pleading that the hole was a mere negative

[3] David Hume. Dialogues concerning Natural Religion, part x.

absence of matter. The logical principle to which this points is that a negative is always also a positive. A hole is a positive existence. If something is a part of our experience, it is thereby proved to exist, whether we choose to call it positive or negative. We may say that darkness is the absence of light, but the darkness of the night is just as much a positively experienced fact as is the light of the day. Rest may be represented as the absence of motion, cold as the absence of heat. But they are positive parts of experience. Cold can kill a man. And when the physician orders rest for the patient, he is not ordering nothing.

Another common device for pretending that evil and pain are not real existences has been to represent them as due to the "partial" view of the universe which is inevitable to finite minds. Evil and pain would be seen to disappear if we could see the world as a whole—just as the ugliness of some dull grey blob of paint in a picture, when it is looked at by itself, is seen to disappear in, and indeed to contribute to, the beauty of the picture when it is seen as a whole. Bishop Berkeley went so far as to write that "the very blemishes and defects of nature are not without their uses. They make an agreeable variety and augment the beauty of the rest of creation as shadows in a picture serve to set off the brighter parts." [4] One feels at once what a hollow mockery this is. To the cultured Irish bishop, comfortable in his palace, the terrible agony of the cancer patient, or of the man burned alive in a fire, might seem to make in the world "an agreeable variety," but they are not this to the man who suffers them. And even if the appearance of evil is due to a partial view of the world, it will still be the case that the partial view itself really exists and is an evil existence.

To take another example, let us consider how the statement that God is love will fare at the hands of the philosophic sceptic. We need not consider the contradiction between this belief and the existence of pain in the world since

[4] *Principles of Human Knowledge*, Section 152.

that was, in effect, the point of the last example. We will suppose that the sceptic takes this time a different approach. We are, of course, taking the proposition that God is love in its literal meaning, and not merely as symbolic. Taken so, the doctrine implies that God is a person, a mind, a consciousness; and these words, too, must be taken in their literal meanings. Love is some kind of emotion or feeling or attitude or desire or at least a purpose—perhaps the purpose to act in a certain way, for instance, to achieve the happiness and good of created beings. But can any of this be literally true of God? Only, apparently, if God be thought of as a finite centre of consciousness, one mind among other minds. This mind, God, loves that mind, a human soul. But apart from this, to attribute emotions to God conflicts with the very definite religious intuition that God is *unchanging*. He is "without shadow of turning." The intuition of the unchanging character of God finds expression in the lines of the hymn:

"O strength and stay upholding all creation
Who ever dost thyself *unmoved abide*." (italics mine)

There is no question that this cannot be evaded by saying that the unchangeable nature of God is a mere metaphysical speculation. It makes its appearance in one form or another in every higher religion, proving that it is an essential part of the religious consciousness. But it is logically incompatible with the conception of God as a mind or consciousness having emotions, feelings, or attitudes. For it is of the essence of a mind to move, to change, to be active. It is a stream of conscious states in time. And if we say that this is not true of God's mind, that we are only using analogies from human consciousness and experience to help us understand something which is in fact quite different, if we say this, we may be saying what is true, but we have abandoned the literal interpretation of God as a mind, and have admitted that the attribution of mind to Him is only a metaphor. We have given up literal interpretation in favor of symbolical interpretation. This will be true in regard to any psychological terms we use of Him, such as "mind," "consciousness," "thought," "purpose," "love," or the names of any other emotions or psychic states.

What we have here in reality is a particular case of the general contradiction between the negative divine and the positive divine. It is part of the positive divine to affirm activity of God, the creative activity which results in the existence of the world, as well as those activities which are involved in guiding and controlling the world and in the loving care of His children. This is the dynamic conception of God. But it is an essential part of the negative divine that God is wholly inactive. This appears as the concept of His "unchangeableness." This conflicts with the dynamic conception, yet both the dynamic and the passive are equally necessary elements in the religious consciousness. The one corresponds to the Being, the other to the Non-Being, of God. In Sankara the contradiction between the two conceptions seeks resolution in the establishment in his theory of two Brahmans, the "higher" and the "lower," the former quality-less, passionless, motionless, inactive, the latter carrying God's creative activity. In Christianity the problem is just as real, though it is not so glaringly obvious. It makes its appearance in the unchangeableness of God, which implies inactivity, on the one hand, and His activity of creation, guidance, control, love of man, and the rest, on the other. The same conflict of the active and the passive causes the Greek splitting of the divine into God and the demi-urge, the latter to exercise the creative activity.

The conception of God as a mind or a person in a literal sense, as well as conflicting with His unchangeableness, also contradicts His infinity. For no mind can be infinite, in the ordinary sense of the word infinite, which means the mathematical infinite. For a mind, as we have seen, necessarily changes. But that which changes cannot be infinite. The notion of change implies that the changing thing possesses a character at one time which it lacks at another. That which changes from green to red lacks green when it is red, and lacks red when it is green. But that which lacks anything is not mathematically infinite. Nor will it help us to suppose that the mind of God, though it contains emotions and ideas, is unchanging in that these emotions and ideas are always the same; for instance, that His love is an unswerving love always for the same objects. Though such a mind is a psychological impossibility in our actual world, it is not perhaps a logical self-contradiction. But apart from the fact that such a conception of God is a mere metaphysical abstraction, lacking in any basis in religious intuition, it is in any case logically incompatible with the activity of God.

The activity of God conflicts just as much with the conception of the religious infinite. For change is the passing from this to that, and in the unity and infinity of God there is no distinction of this from that.

What lesson do we learn from this excursion into scepticism? What it shows is that *all* religious language must be taken as symbolical, and not as literal. The moment you take your religious doctrine as literal, you find that it results in contradictions, for instance between the goodness of God and the evil in the world, or between God's unchangeableness and His activity, or between His personality and His infinity. These contradictions are the stock in trade of the sceptic. His business consists in pointing them out. He always necessarily wins because the contradictions are real and cannot be evaded by any subterfuges. The common defense put up by religious men has always consisted in vainly trying to explain the contradictions away, which cannot be done. This is why conventional Christian apologetics always appear so weak. They evade difficulties by pretences such as that pain and evil do not really exist. It is in this way that the literal interpretation of religious doctrines has scepticism as its necessary and inevitable result.

We are thus again forced to concede that the Ultimate is beyond all conception, that whatever concept we use to try to understand it leads the mind at once into logical contradictions, that our words and our language can never do more than evoke in us dim intuitions of what lies beyond all thought. This is the meaning of the negative divine, and this is the justification of the symbolical interpretation of religious language.

We also learn from these considerations that there is no halfway house between literalism and symbolicism, such as is perhaps fondly desired by the distracted and perplexed religious thinkers of our day. We have seen that their usual procedure is to stick doggedly to the literal so long as they can, and to admit symbolic interpretation only when they are forced by the scientific or philosophical sceptic to do so. In order to do this they set up a distinction between the essential and the inessential doctrines of religion, which distinction however they are unable to define and therefore unable to defend. This procedure has some temporary success so long as it is only the conflict of religion with science which is considered. But it is a useless strategy as against philosophic scepticism which attacks what these men cannot avoid, so long as they remain with one foot in the literalist camp, regarding as essential doctrines, such as the personality and love of God. The point of our criticism has been to show that this stance, half literalist, half symbolicist, cannot be maintained. For the kind of scepticism of which we have given examples shows that even the so-called essential doctrines of religion have also to be admitted to be symbolical only.

It follows that all propositions about God are false, *if they are understood literally*. This will apply to the proposition "God exists" as well as to any other. It will also apply to the proposition "God does not exist." God is above both existence and non-existence.

This result should not be either surprising or alarming if

we remember our previous conclusions. God is not to be apprehended, we saw, by concepts, but only by that intuition wherein the distinction between subject and object is transcended. But this at once implies that all *propositions* about God, including "God is" and "God is not," are false. For all propositions operate through concepts. And all propositions are the work of the logical intellect. The same conclusion is reached as a result of the statement that the intuition of God is transcendent of the subject-object division. For "existence" involves that division. That which exists is that which is an object, or possible object, of thought. Finally, the same conclusions are implied by the infinity of God. For the infinite is "that than which there is no other." But to exist means to be one of the many things which stand in relation to one another and which, thus systematically related, constitute the universe.

We are not at the end of our troubles when we have decided that all religious language is symbolic. We have to ask what is the nature and justification of religious symbolism.

There is a condition which attaches to all use of metaphor, myth, allegory, analogy, ideogram—all of which terms we include here under the general head of symbolic language. The condition is that both the symbol and that which it symbolizes should be present to the mind of the user of the symbol. If this is not the case the symbolism becomes meaningless. It becomes what is sometimes called "mere" metaphor.

Philosophers frequently accuse each other of indulging in "mere" metaphor. We have to ask what this means, what is the fault which these words imply. It cannot be maintained that all metaphor is as such illegitimate. For metaphor is inwoven in all except the most rudimentary use of language, and we could scarcely express any thoughts, except the barest and most simple, without the use of metaphor. Thus we have to inquire what is the distinction between the legitimate and the illegitimate use of metaphor which is implied in the charge that some philosophical language is "mere" metaphor.

Symbolism is a relation to which there must be two terms. One term is the sensuous image or picture which is the metaphor or symbol. The other term is the thing or truth which the symbol or image stands for and represents. The condition for the valid use of symbolic language is that both terms should be in some sense present to the mind. Both terms must be in some way known. If this is not the case, if only one term of the relation, namely the symbol, is present to the mind, then the symbol is meaningless, and we have the condition which is described as "mere" metaphor.

It is not necessary that the meaning of the symbolic language, or symbolizandum, should be *clearly* before the mind. It may be only dimly and faintly apprehended in the borderlands of consciousness, or perhaps in the sub-conscious. It is because this is often the case that we usually make use of symbolic language. The symbol is a clear picture in the mind, but the other term of the relation is not. It is only vaguely glimpsed. The symbol helps us to drag it into the light of consciousness, to make it clearer, or at least the symbol stands for us in the place of a clear understanding of it. But, clearly or dimly, the symbolizandum must be apprehended for the language to have any meaning.

When Shakespeare speaks of "taking arms against a sea of troubles," in this metaphor we have both terms of the symbolic relation before the mind. The picture of the sea is the symbol. The other term, the meaning, is perhaps the multitudinous character of the troubles—like the multitudinous waves of the sea—or their alarming or overwhelming nature. In Bunyan's *Pilgrim's Progress* the story itself is the symbol, while its meaning is the life of the Christian in the world with its constant battle against temptation. Both are present to the mind throughout the reading of the book—that is, if the book is understood. In Plato's myth of

the cave the ascent of the prisoners to the sunlight represents
a turning of the mind from the concrete and sensuous to
the universal and the abstract.

Will religious symbolism stand this test? Is the meaning
of the symbols before the mind, however dimly? Or is the
meaning side of the symbolic relation a total blank, so that
we have the condition called "mere" metaphor?

The difficulty of this question lies in the fact that the
condition of legitimate symbolism seems to imply that it
must always be possible to translate the symbolic language
into literal language, and that in religious symbolism this is
not possible. When we say that it must be possible to translate
the symbolism into literal language, this does not mean that
it must be easy to do so. Where the literal meaning is only
dimly apprehended, translation may be in fact so difficult
that we fail to accomplish it. To say that it must be possible
means only that the translation into literal language must
be at least theoretically possible. The meaning of the symbol
must be of such a nature that it *could* be expressed in literal
language, if we could get it clear enough and could find
the right words. But that any such translation of religious
symbolism into literal language is not even theoretically possible is what is meant by the ineffability of God or of the
mystic experience.

We may put the same difficulty in another way. We have
a symbolic proposition about God, for example, that God
is love. To translate this metaphor into literal language could
only mean to state another proposition in which the word
"love" would be replaced by some word which is not metaphorical. But we should still have a proposition. And what
our analysis has shown is that *all* propositions about God are
false, or in other words that there cannot exist any true literal
propositions about Him. Are we not forced by this into
admitting that religious symbolism is "mere" metaphor, that
it is illegitimate, that it has no meaning? And will not this
mean that the road to God—if indeed to speak of God has

now any meaning—is wholly barred to the human soul? Can
God be to us anything more than an empty Unknowable—
the common position of agnosticism?

The difficulty may be put in another way. It is commonly
said that religious language, though not literally true, affords
us "glimpses" or "hints" of the nature of the divine. These
words "glimpses" and "hints" tend, by their vagueness, to
hide from the religious man the real difficulty. The point is
that unless the symbolism is to be mere metaphor, there
must be, directly present to the mind the actual nature of
the Godhead symbolized as well as the symbol itself. It
means that God Himself must be in some way directly apprehended, and not merely indirectly through the symbol.
No doubt this direct vision of the divine may be very dim,
wavering, and of course utterly imperfect, and this is no
doubt what is meant to be conveyed by the words "glimpse"
and "hint." But there must be some direct vision, otherwise
the symbolism will be empty verbiage.

But there is a way out of this impasse. It is only to the
conceptual intellect that the road to God is barred. It is not
the case that God, the positive God, the God of love, cannot
be apprehended at all. He cannot be apprehended by the
concept. This is the very meaning of the "incomprehensibility" of God, as also of the negative divine, God as Nothing, the Void. But He does reveal Himself to man, not
negatively but positively, in that form of human consciousness which, for lack of a better term, we have called intuition.

This fact provides the solution of our difficulty about religious symbolism. The symbolic proposition about God
does not stand for another proposition—a literal one—about
God. It stands for and represents the mystical experience
itself. It is not a proposition about God which is symbolized,
but God Himself as He is actually found and experienced
"in the heart," that is, in the mystical vision. And this experience, thus symbolized, is actually present to the mind

in the form of an intuition, though not in the form of a conceptualizable representation.

When the symbolic language provides a hint of the nature of God, what is happening is that the symbol stands before the intellect or imagination, while God Himself is directly present to intuition. Thus both terms of the symbolic relation are present to the mind, if the mind be understood as including the whole soul, both intellect and intuition.

Does this mean that it is only the great mystics who can know God, that He can be apprehended only in that abnormal ecstasy which is said to be the condition of mystic vision? Does it mean that to the rest of us the road to God is barred, and that we can know of Him only on hearsay? If so, mankind would be in a sorry plight, and religion no more than a traveler's tale of some far off land which most of us could never hope to see. We must hold, on the contrary, that God can, and indeed does, make His presence directly felt in the consciousness even of the humblest. And this necessitates our believing that intuition exists in all of us, that it is a perfectly normal mode of consciousness. The fact that some men do not recognize its existence in themselves, or may even entirely deny its possibility, is no argument against this view. We do not have to know psychology, to understand how the mind operates, in order to use our mental powers, any more than we have to know the structure of our digestive organs in order to digest our food. Many a man uses logic who does not understand the theory of the syllogism. Many a man uses concepts without knowing what a concept is. Thus, too, men use whatever capacity they have for mystical intuition without being aware of it or knowing how it operates. Nor is it an objection to say that mystical intuition is supposed to imply that the division between subject and object is transcended, and that we are not aware of any such process going on in ourselves. For again we are not necessarily aware of the nature of our own mental processes. And certainly we must hold that, although the great mystic is one in whom the vision of God is so clear that he is able to detect therein that transcendence of the subject-object distinction of which he tells us, in most of us it is so dim and unformed, so mixed with other and irrelevant states of mind—with sense-apprehensions and thoughts of other things—so sunk also as it may be below the level of our conscious minds, that we fail entirely to understand its true character. Nor, finally, is it any objection to our view that for most of us there is no "ecstasy" or "trance" involved. For in the first place it is by no means certain that any such abnormal conditions are necessary even for the great mystic. And in the second place, even if they are, why should we be surprised at this or at our own lack of any such ecstasy? Our supposition is that mystic intuition exists in all men, but that in the great mystic it is developed in an abnormal degree. If this is so, one would expect that he, though not we, would become so rapt and absorbed in his vision, that consciousness of other things and of the world around him might drop away entirely for the time-being. And presumably this would be the condition which might be described as an ecstasy or even a trance.

The results of this chapter may be summarized. The contradiction of the Being and the Non-Being of God is resolved by the discovery that His positive nature is revealed in religious intuition, but is veiled to the conceptual intellect, to which He is incomprehensible; and that it is this blankness and nothingness to the intellect which, as the negative divine, give rise to those expressions of God as the Void, or as Nothing, which are familiar in the literature of mysticism. This implies that all religious and theological language is symbolic, since any literal application of words and concepts to the "nameless" God is blocked by the conceptual character of all thinking and speaking. There is no possibility of a half-way position in which some propositions about God shall be symbolic and others literal. But religious symbolism has its own special character which differs from all ordinary use of metaphorical language. The condition of legitimate metaphor is that both terms of the symbolic relation, the metaphor or symbol and that for which it stands, should be present to the mind. In non-religious symbolic language this means that the symbolic proposition must be translateable into a literal proposition. In religious symbolism this is impossible, because any literal proposition about God would involve the conceptualization of that which is above all conceptions. But religious symbolism is not on this account mere metaphor, because that which is symbolized is not a proposition about God but the direct apprehension of His presence in religious or mystic intuition. This intuition is not the exclusive possession of recognized mystics, but is found in all men in greater or lesser degree. Thus both the symbol and the symbolizandum are present to the mind—the condition of legitimate metaphor—the symbol in the form of the religious doctrine or proposition, the reality symbolized in the form of the mind's intuition.

CHAPTER 5 TIME AND ETERNITY

THE CONCLUSIONS REACHED IN THE LAST CHAPTER POSE FOR us, it will be found, a new set of problems. For the critic of these conceptions may argue in the following manner. It is supposed, he will say, that there exists in mystical intuition a kind of experience which is inherently incapable of being conceptualized. But this is, in the first place, impossible. And in the second place, even if it were possible, it would imply that that experience is so completely cut off from the rest of human experience that the two will stand in no relation at all. This in turn will imply that God is so "utterly other" that there is no relation whatever between God and the world. Further unacceptable implications will also be involved, for instance, that there cannot be any relation of similarity between the experience of one mystic and that of another, nor even between two mystical experiences of the same person. All this is not only unacceptable, but strictly unthinkable, inconceivable, and therefore impossible.

We must examine these contentions with great care. We shall find that they lead us to the conception of two distinct dimensions or orders of being, the order of time and the order of eternity.

Why, first of all, is it supposed that there could not be an experience which is inherently incapable of being enmeshed in concepts? The reason given will be that if there be any experience, datum, or thing of any kind whatever before the mind, it must be related in some way to the other experiences of the same mind. It must at least be either like or unlike those experiences, that is, it must bear to them the relations of similarity or dissimilarity. It must also be distinguishable from them, that is, it must bear to them the relation of difference. But whatever has relations is conceptualizable, since to know a thing's relations is to know its concept. More precisely, to have a concept of anything means

no more than to know to what other things it bears the relation of similarity. The concept of a triangle is formed by
noting the points in which all triangles resemble one another,
namely in being bounded by three straight lines. Thus if the
mystic knows the resemblances between the various occasions on which he has the mystic experience, and their differences from his ordinary experiences of daily life, he has already in this knowledge a concept of them. This is reflected
in the very fact that he uses such words as "mystical," "numinous," and even "experience" of them. These are all concepts. They all connote resemblances and differences between his mystical and his other experiences. Indeed even
to say that his experience is unconceptualizable is to apply
a concept to it, since it connotes a resemblance between different occasions of the experience, and a difference between
it and other experiences. If a man could have one set of experiences without any relation to his other experiences, this
would mean that the two sets of experiences could not be
within the unity of the same mind. Moreover, if there were
a being or existence out of all relation to the other beings
and existences of the world, then it could not be part of the
universe, since the universe simply *is* the totality of all inter-
related and inter-connected things.

We shall have to point out later that God is not a *part*
of the universe, one thing among other things and standing
in relations with them. For this would involve His otherness
to them and would accordingly destroy His infinity. For
the moment we may make a partial answer to the above
criticism by pointing out that it relies on a use of the word
"experience" which is inapplicable to the case in hand. By
an experience we ordinarily mean something which is before the mind or present to it. This involves a distinction
between the mind and its experience or object. Thus the
color or smell is "there," and I, who cognize it, am different
from it. Moreover one color is like another, and is unlike
a smell. In all such experiences, therefore, the concept comes

into play. But the mystic experience is not of this kind. For there is in it no division of mind from its object, nor any other distinction between this and that. It is a flawless indivisible unity, which gives no foothold for the concept. This is what it is *in itself*. It is true that, if it is looked at *from the outside*, as for example it is by the mystic himself when he returns to the level of his every day or temporal experience, then it will be different from that ordinary experience, and will be conceptually distinguished as the mystical from the non-mystical. In short, conceptualization implies the distinction between subject and object as well as other distinctions, and the religious experience is nonconceptualizable because no such distinctions exist in it.

But it will be said that all this implies a God who stands in no relation to the world at all, and for obvious reasons this is impossible. We have therefore to discuss the problem of the relation of God to the world. Now it follows from all that has been said that when we speak of God having some relation to the world our language must be symbolic only. "God is related to the world" is a proposition about God, and is therefore false if it is taken in a literal sense. That no predicates apply to God is a statement which must be understood as including relations among predicates. To see that this must be so we have only to see that the attribution of relations to God leads to the same sort of contradictions and absurdities as does the attribution of qualities. It is inconsistent, for example, with God's infinity. For a relation implies at least two terms between which the relation holds. In this case the two terms would be God and the world. But if the world is other than God, then God is limited by the world, and is not infinite. He is not "that than which there is no other."

We may look at the various attempts which have been made in different religions to state or conceive the relations between God and the world. We shall find that, if taken literally, they are all impossible and absurd. Space relations,

time relations, and causal relations have been those which
have been most commonly implied in these conceptions.
Men began perhaps with spatial relations. God was above
the sky, above the stars, or outside the spherical universe.
It would be generally recognized today that any such conception could be only symbolical. To this succeeded the
notion that God is "omnipresent." This was taken quite literally by Newton who thought that space was God's "sen-
sorium," that God is spread all through it, so that the planets
are actually moving through the space occupied by God's
mind. No doubt the metaphor of omnipresence has a meaning, but it can hardly be anything so crude as this. We should
hold that it is a metaphor for God's infinity, according to
which conception space cannot be outside of God—that is,
other to God—nor can any part of it be outside Him. Evidently we cannot conceive the relation between God and
the world as a spatial one.

A time relation between God and the world finds expression in the phrase that God is "before all the worlds,"
and is also implied by the common conception that God
created the world at some moment in time. However we
conceive it, a temporal relation of God to the world puts
God in the time-stream, makes Him part of the natural order, a temporal being. According to some theologians, the
conclusion that God is in the time-stream is not to be drawn,
because the creation of time was part of the creation of the
world. God created time, along with the world which exists
in it. But this obviously involves contradictions. If the creation was a temporal act at all—and so it must be conceived
if we are to take any of these ideas literally—then there was
a moment *in* time at which the world came into being, and
before that there was a time when it was not in being.

A causal relation between God and the world has been,
on the whole, the most common conception. It is implied by
the doctrine of creation. God is the cause, the world is the
effect. Since a causal relation means a succession of cause

and effect in time, this involves the same difficulties as those set out in the last paragraph. It either places God in the time-stream, or it involves contradictions in its concept of time. It also destroys the infinity of God, since in any causal relation the effect is other than the cause.[1] And if it be said that God's causality is to be understood differently from the ordinary causality which we find in the created world, as for example the causing of ice by cold, this is to admit our point, namely that none of these relations, temporal, spatial, or causal, as applied to God's relation to the world, can be taken literally, but that all such language is symbolical in character.

In Hinduism God's relation to the world is not conceived as creation, but as manifestation. This, however, can be understood only by the use of some metaphor. God is not then "before" the world, but "behind" it. He is that which is behind the veil of Maya, though possibly He shines through the veil as a lamp shines through the lamp shade which hides it. But "behind" is a spatial metaphor just as "before" is a temporal one. Sometimes, indeed, the notion of manifestation is conceived by means of the ideas conveyed by the words "form" or "aspect." Brahman takes on the form or aspect of being the world, as carbon takes on the form of diamond, or as energy takes on the forms of light, heat, or electricity. Plainly all such ideas are metaphorical. If taken literally, they contradict the infinity of Brahman. Brahman is "the One without a second." Therefore the world cannot be other than God, even in the sense in which a form of something is other than the thing when it is not in that form. The world, in Hinduism, *is* Brahman. But also

[1] It is true that there are identity theories of causation, according to which cause and effect are identical. But they are patently absurd. They are compelled to maintain that cause and effect are different "forms" or "aspects" of the same identical thing. But then the difference between cause and effect reappears as a difference of form or aspect. There may be some intelligible sense in which charcoal and diamond are two forms of carbon, but that charcoal is not the same thing as diamond will be discovered if you try to sell it to a jeweller.

the world is *not* Brahman, because the appearance, the illusion, is not the reality, because the world is in time and space, while Brahman is "above time, above space," and because the world is marked by manyness and division of one thing from another, whereas there is no division in the being of Brahman. Thus the contradiction involved in the conception of manifestation, if taken in any literal way, is explicit.

Thus all conceptions of the relation between God and the world, which have been commonly affirmed by the religious consciousness, must be taken as no more than metaphors, since to take them literally leads to contradictions. And the conclusion is that the very idea of relation, as holding between God and the world, is metaphorical. It might perhaps be said that God may have some relation to the world other than those which we have just examined, or even some relation of which the human mind is incapable of conceiving. What we are striving to show, however, is that to assert any kind of relation at all between God and the world, known or unknown, conceivable or inconceivable, is of necessity to use language which cannot be literal but must be metaphorical only. For any relation whatever, in as much as it would imply that the world is other than God, would destroy His infinity. It would also conflict with that intuition of God's relationlessness which is a part and parcel of the religious consciousness everywhere. The same conclusion is implied by the conception of the negative divine, which, as we have seen, is an essential element of the religious consciousness. For according to that conception, no predicates, and therefore no relational predicates, can be applied to the Ultimate.

The conclusion is that any proposition asserting any relation between God and the world is a symbolic proposition and not a literal truth. If the word relation be taken in a literal sense, then God has no relation to the world. And this is what, on other grounds, we ought to have expected. For if God were related to the things in the world, then He would Himself be one among other things. He would be a part of the universe, a part of the natural order. He would be a natural, not a supernatural, being. For the natural order is to be defined as the totality of things—whether these things be minds or material things—which are linked into a single system by relations. Yet though we may say that the word relation, as used of God, is a metaphor, we are bound—unless we are to be charged with the fault of using "mere" metaphor—to say what this metaphor means in terms of the actual religious experience. What do the metaphors of creation, manifestation, being before the world, or behind it, mean? And the answers to these questions have still to be found.

But in order to develop our conceptions we will continue for the moment to speak in metaphorical language. We will take our metaphor from the lines of T. S. Eliot:

> "To apprehend
> The point of intersection of the timeless
> With time is an occupation for the saint." [2]

There are two orders, the natural order which is the order of time, and the divine order, which is the order of eternity. In the moment of mystic illumination the two orders intersect, so that that moment belongs to both orders. The image of the intersecting straight lines breaks down in one respect. Two physical straight lines intersect at only one point, and then diverge. But we have to suppose that, in some way, every moment of time is an intersection of the divine order with the natural order. But if every moment of time is thus in fact traversed by the line of the divine dimension, it is only in the rare moment of illumination in the life of the saint that this is clearly apprehended and fully realized.

Within that single moment of time are enclosed all eternity and all infinity. This is the meaning of Blake's words:

[2] *The Dry Salvages.*

"To see the world in a grain of sand,
    And a heaven in a wild flower,
Hold infinity in the palm of your hand,
    And eternity in an hour."

It is a commonplace that eternity is not an endless prolongation of time, has nothing to do with time. Eternity is a characteristic of the mystical experience. The word eternity doubtless meant originally endlessness of time, which must count, therefore, as its literal meaning. But in its religious and metaphysical use it is a metaphor for the characteristic of the experience. For in that experience time drops away and is no more seen. The same is true of infinity. This does not mean the endlessness of a series. The mystic illumination is infinite in itself because there is nothing outside it, because there is within it no this or that, no limiting otherness. And the word infinity, originally and literally meaning the endlessness of a series, is now used as a metaphor for this. And that the experience is eternal, that is to say timeless, also follows from the fact that there are in it no divisions or relations. For there cannot be time where there are no divisions and relations of "before" and "after." We have spoken of the infinity and eternity of the divine moment in the experience of the saint. But we may also speak in the same terms of the infinity and eternity of God. For these two are identical.

The eternal moment, being a point of intersection, can be looked at either from within or from without. Since it belongs to both orders, it is both temporal and eternal. Looked at internally—that is as the mystic himself sees it in that moment—it is infinite and eternal. Looked at from the outside—as it is seen, not only by all of us in our normal consciousness, but by the mystic himself when he has passed out of it into the time-order, and looks back upon it in memory—looked at thus externally it is a moment in time. From within it is God. For it is not a consciousness *of* God, a divided consciousness wherein the mystic as subject stands over against Deity as object. It is the immanence of God Himself in the soul. But, as it is looked at from the outside, its content is merely a passing state of the mind of the mystic.

Naturalism is the philosophy which asserts the sole reality of the natural order, and denies the reality of the divine order. That is, it looks at the divine moment only externally. The content, the inner filling, of the moment is then for it illusion. Not that it denies that the moment occurs as a fact in time. Not that it denies that the saint has the experience which he says he has. But the experience is seen as merely subjective, that is, illusory. God is then an illusion.

But there is also necessarily an opposite kind of illusionism. For if we take our stand within the moment itself, it is then the world, the natural order, which is illusion. For the content of the moment is the infinite, and outside the infinite there is nothing. The world is therefore nothing. The content of the moment is also eternity, and there is therefore outside it no time. Hence arises that acosmism, that denial of the reality of the world, which is associated with mysticism and with those systems of metaphysics which have their origin in mysticism. Acosmism reaches its highest point in the religious philosophies of India with their doctrine of the world as maya. In the west it appears in philosophies like that of Bradley. Bradley is only dimly aware of the mystical character of his own philosophy, and supposes himself to be in general a rationalist. But his remark in the introduction to his book *Appearance and Reality* that philosophy is "a satisfaction of what may be called the mystical side of our nature," reveals the secret sources of his thought. For him time and space and the world are only "appearance," not reality. Appearance is a word which is not so extreme as illusion. Yet it is only a lesser degree of the same denial of the reality of the world. All philosophies which declare that time, space, and the world, are unreal, or half real, or phenomenal, or appearances, or illusion, have their roots in mysticism. For the proposition "the world is unreal" is a mystical proposition, not a factual proposition. It derives from the mystical vision of the eternal and infinite moment outside which there is no other and therefore no world, no space, no time. But, for the majority of so-called and self-styled rationalistic philosophers, the divine moment is so deeply buried in their sub-conscious that they are only dimly aware of it and suppose that their conclusions are the result of logical argument. In them the mystical wells up from the depths to the surface consciousness, where it is then rationalized.

The mystic lives in both orders, that of eternity and that of time. He passes from one to the other. This is also true of other men in the degree in which the mystic consciousness is developed in them. But this dual existence gives rise to confusion of the one order with the other. For the pure mystic consciousness there is no world at all. It is pure illusion. For the pure natural consciousness there is no God and no divine. They are entirely illusory. But because men live in both orders the two extremes of illusionism, atheism and acosmism, are rarely met with—though of course atheism is much the commoner. When the great mystic passes back from the order of eternity into the order of time, the world which has been, in that pure moment, a total illusion, reappears and forces itself upon him. It again asserts its reality. Yet the memory and influence of that tremendous moment are still upon him, and cause him to attribute to the world a shadowy half-reality. Hence arises the notion of *degrees* of reality, which is so common in philosophies like those of the Vedanta, Bradley, and Hegel, and which is so puzzling to the naturalistically-minded man. According to this conception, one thing can be more real than another. Only the Ultimate—which is the content of the pure mystic moment —is absolutely real. Other things are more or less real according as they are nearer or further away from the divine order.

Since there are two orders of being, there are therefore

two solutions of every metaphysical problem, the naturalistic solution and the mystical solution. Each is, in its own right, absolute and final. They seem to contradict one another, but this contradiction occurs only as a result of the confusion between the two orders. If the divine order is, in the minds of men, as it almost always is, brought down into the natural order and *supposed to be a part of it*, then a contradiction arises. God is thought to be one being among other beings, though He may be the cause of these other beings. His existence then becomes a superstition against which the scientist, the naturalist, or the philosopher has to fight. This being cannot be found anywhere among other beings either by telescopes or by rational arguments or inferences from the other beings. This confusion, this taking of the eternal order for a part of the natural order, is the source of all scepticism, and of the whole conflict between science, or scientific naturalism, and religion. For as soon as the divine is thus put within the natural order it is seen that it cannot be found there, that it does not exist there; and so its reality is denied. All efforts to compromise between science (or philosophy) and religion are puerile attempts to divide the world of existence, the natural order, into areas, of which one is to be assigned to science, the other to religion. The true way to resolve the conflict is to realize the difference of the two orders. It is then possible to give to each the *whole* of what it claims and not merely some ungenerously clipped off portion.

In this conception of the intersection of the divine and natural there is a point which is at present obscure. We cannot hold that the divine intersects the natural only at that one point which is the consciousness of the saint. We must surely believe that the divine interpenetrates the natural everywhere. The divine order must intersect the temporal order at every moment of time and at every point of space. For this is demanded by the intuition of the "omnipresence" of God. We cannot at present see how this is possible. We see how the intersection occurs in the moment of human mystical illumination, and since this moment is not only present in the great mystic, but in all men, we may say that we see—at least dimly—how it occurs throughout that area of the natural world which is the human mind. But what is to be said of animals and plants? And what of inanimate objects, such as rocks and metals? Mr. Gandhi is reported to have said "God is in the stone." This is, of course, religious language, and is therefore symbolical. (To suppose that it is literally true would mean that God is in the stone in the same sense as silica or feldspar are in the stone.) But if it is not to be mere metaphor, some symbolized meaning must be given to it. And the question is, what meaning? Of how God is in the human heart we know something from our own inner experience. But how is God in the stone? How does the eternal order intersect the natural order at the space-time point where the stone is?

It may be said that God's being in the stone is a pantheistic doctrine, not acceptable to Christianity. But this would be a mistake. Pantheism is the error that God is *only* in the world, and that He is not transcendent of it. And if we reject pantheism it should not be on the ground that we deny God's immanence everywhere and in everything, but rather on the ground that although God is immanent everywhere, at every point of space and moment of time—which is the meaning of His omnipresence—He is also transcendent. And, in the conception of a divine intersection of the natural order, the immanence of God is represented by the assertion that the intersection takes place at every point, while His transcendence is represented by the fact that the divine and eternal is a wholly different order or dimension from the natural.

Hence we still have the question how God can be in the stone. We do not, I believe, know enough to give any sort of confident answer. I will give the answer which I believe to be true, while admitting its speculative character. It seems probable that, as the pan-psychistic philosophy of Whitehead has suggested, there is no distinction, except one of degree, between the organic and inorganic, or between life and mind. Alexander's doctrine of emergent evolution supposed the following levels of emergence—space-time, inorganic matter, life (found without consciousness in plants), and mind or consciousness. This may well be correct, but Alexander supposed an absolute break between each of the levels. The organic philosophy of Whitehead would suppose, on the contrary, that there is no such break. There is continuity. The common thread running throughout the series is life. All things are living. Even an electron is a very low-grade organism, a living being. The essence of its being, as of every being, is feeling or experience, although in the pre-animal levels the feelings and experiences are blind and unconscious. This is supported by many analogies, and also by some "scientific" considerations. For instance, it makes possible an explanation of how life appeared on the earth out of previous "inorganic" existences. There is also the fact that in the virus we have a being which exhibits some of the characteristics of the organic and some of the characteristics of the inorganic, suggesting that it is not possible to draw a sharp line between the two. We may then well suppose that what we call the deadness of inorganic existences is but a deep hypnotic sleep of their consciousness.

If we combine this suggestion with another, which has already been made in these pages, we can perhaps obtain some light on our problem. This other suggestion was that, in those men who are not what are commonly called mystics, the divine moment lies in the sub-conscious, far down in some, nearer to the surface in others. In the great mystic it has emerged into the full light of conscious mentality. In common men it exists not far from the surface, so that it stirs the surface and appears there as dim religious feeling, which can be evoked and enhanced—that is, drawn nearer to the surface—by the symbolic language of religion and especially by the language of the mystic. Experiments in hypnosis plainly show not only that there are the conscious and the unconscious, but that there are also levels of unconsciousness. We easily accept the fact that there are degrees of consciousness. A man's mind may be alertly conscious or only dimly aware of things. A state of dreamy or drowsy awareness passes by degrees into sleep. But we are apt to suppose that unconsciousness is without degrees, that it is simply a total absence of consciousness. But even the common fact that one sleep may be deeper than another should dissipate this belief. And the facts of hypnosis make it certain that it is false. There are deeper and deeper levels of hypnosis, greater and lesser darknesses, darkness below darkness. It may well be that what we call the life of the plant is but a level of the hypnotic sleep of consciousness lower than is ever found in the animal, and that in the metal and the rock the darkness is deeper still, but that, even there, a blind unconscious mentality exists. Perhaps, then, in the plant and the metal the divine moment exists, utterly submerged. The point of intersection is there, buried in the blackness of the night of that metallic consciousness, or that plant consciousness, which we can only dimly apprehend as akin to hypnotic or sleep states in ourselves. And there, too, perhaps the eternal moment awaits that evolutionary liberation from the darkness, that passage into the light, which has already come in some degree to man, and, in a supreme degree, to mystic man.

We may now try to answer some of the questions which, as we saw, were pressing upon us. What is the meaning of the metaphor of intersection? This intersection means precisely what the eternal moment is experienced to be. It is one and the same human consciousness which experiences both the temporal or natural world and that eternal and infinite order which is disclosed in mystical illumination. Thus this identity of eternity with a temporal moment is an actual experienced fact, and this fact is what is metaphorically represented by the image of intersection.

What relation does one eternal moment bear to another—whether the two which we compare belong to the mind-stream of the same man, or to the mind-streams of two different men? To this, as to all religious or metaphysical questions, there are two different answers, according as we take our stand within the moment or outside it. From the outside, we shall say that one such moment bears to another the relation of resemblance, and also no doubt some relations of non-resemblance. Thus what one mystic reports resembles what another reports in most ways, but there may be some differences. This result seems to lead to embarrassment, because it introduces relations into what purports to be relationless, and thereby renders the mystic experience a proper subject matter for concepts and predicates. For to say that experience A is like experience B is to assert a common element as between them and therefore the possibility of a concept. And it is in this way that in fact we get such concepts as "mystical" and "numinous."

But obviously if we thus start our inquiry from the naturalistic standpoint we come out with a naturalistic conclusion. The eternal moment is then a point in the line of time, and so must be related to other such points. But looked at from within the point, these questions do not arise. Since the point is the infinite and eternal, there is no *other* point to which it can bear a relation. But, it will be said, even the mystic cannot deny that there are other mystics, or that he himself at other times has had, or may have, other mystical experiences, and that there must be relations of likeness or unlikeness between his own different experiences, and between the experiences of different mystics. This is quite true. But it is true because the mystic is himself a thing among other things, a person among other persons, an occupant of the time-order, traveling along with other persons and things in the stream of time. He belongs—as of course all men do and, in some sense, all things—to both orders. And his experience is, from this external standpoint, a point in time for him

as well as for us. But if we persist in asking whether, if we take
our stand within the eternal moment itself, all this must not
still remain true, the answer is, no; because in that experience
there is no subject and no object, and as the mystic is therein
identical with God, so he is therein identical with all other
mystics, and his mystic experience is identical with all other
mystic experiences, whether of himself or another, and this
moment of time is identical with all other moments of time.
And hence there is, from within, no relation at all between
one mystic experience and another, and therefore no likeness or unlikeness, and therefore no concept. The time-order
is a line, and we have thought of the religious moment under
the image of its intersection with another line. But the image
fails, as all images do. For it is only from the external standpoint that there is a multiplicity of religious moments represented by the multiplicity of points in the line. In itself the
eternal moment is single. For it is the one God. It is one self-
identical point; but it is a point which is everywhere, co-
extensive with the universe.

We may now return to the question of God's relation to
the world. Since God and the eternal moment are one, whatever may be said of the relation of the eternal moment to
the world may be said of the relation of God to the world.
In the intersection of the two orders God is the eternal, the
infinite, the divine order. God as He is in Himself, as transcendent, is that order taken alone. God as He is in the world,
as immanent, is the intersection of the two orders. The world
as it is in itself is the time-order taken alone. And as at a point
of intersection there are two coincident points, belonging
each to one of the intersecting lines, which are nevertheless
one point, so God and the world are both two and one, distinct and identical. We find this identity in difference of
God and the world in all those philosophies which have their
source in mysticism. In Bradley's metaphysics the Absolute,
being infinite, has nothing outside it. The world therefore
cannot fall outside it. The world is the Absolute. Neverthe-

less the Absolute is different from the world, for in it there is no space, no time, no relation, no division, these being attributable only to the world. In the Vedanta also Brahman both is, and is not, the world. In the philosophy of Spinoza the attributes, which are the world, *constitute* the Substance. And yet Substance is something other than the attributes.

We may say also that, from the standpoint of time, God is in relation to the world. He is omnipresent in it. But from the standpoint of the eternal, which is the inner view of the divine moment, God has no relations either within Himself or with other beings, or with the world.

The question of the relation of God to the world is, after all, a *question;* that is, it employs words and concepts. Necessarily it speaks the language of "is" and "is not." But God neither is nor is not. Therefore He is neither in relation nor out of relation with the world. All these words "relation," "is," "is not," and indeed all words, belong to the language of the natural order. They are appropriate only to it, have meaning only for it. They are the vocabulary of the natural order. They are the language of distinction, of discrimination, of logic, of propositions, of concepts. Hence the answer to all theological problems is either silence, or metaphors. And the true answer is silence, namely the silence which is God Himself. In other words, one can know God only in the intuitive moment itself, and this moment, this experience, being itself the answer, there is no other. But this intuitive moment is in all men, and not only in the great mystic. Therefore the Zen mystic who, being asked for instruction by his disciples, gives him a slap or a kick, is right—though his manner of giving his instruction may be crude. For he means that the pupil's questions cannot be answered by any words, and the truth can be found only by looking within himself, within the eternal moment of the divine experience which is in him. And whether we choose to call this moment God or Nirvana makes no difference. You ask a question. If the answer is to be in words, these words will be meta-

phors, which will always be untrue. But this does not mean
that there is no answer to the question. It means that the
answer lies in the experience, not in a concept. Nor does
it mean that the metaphors are mere metaphors. For they
symbolize the experience itself, which the disciple has to
find within himself. But the Zen saint is nevertheless in error.
He despises the metaphor, and will not use it. But the metaphor has the power to evoke the experience, that is, to draw
it up from the subliminal toward the upper layers of consciousness. This is why other mystics, though they say that
their experience is ineffable, nevertheless speak to us of it
in many words. Nor is this a contradiction. For they do not
seek by their words to communicate their meaning to us, as
when a man says "this is a house" or "that is a tree." They
seek to evoke a meaning which is already in us. In this sense
mystic or religious language is like poetry or music both of
which call up what is within rather than describe what is
without. The function of religious language is like that of
aesthetic language, and is entirely unlike the function of
scientific language. The failure to understand this is one
cause of the conflict between religion and science. Scientific
language is descriptive, religious language evocative.[3] Hence
if religious language is understood as if it were scientific, it
is taken as describing facts, and these alleged facts are seen,
sooner or later, to be untrue.

We have been considering the divine moment as it is in
itself, as seen from the inside. If now we turn to a consideration of it from the outside, several important conclusions
emerge. It is then a point in the line of time, and there are
other such points. The point will be datable in time. We
can say that the saint had the experience at such and such a
time in such and such a year. It will have space-relations as

[3] This is not the same as saying that religious language is emotive.
For what is evoked, the mystic illumination, is misdescribed if it
is called an emotion. An emotion is thought of as subjective only.
But the illumination transcends the subject-object dualism.

well as time-relations. It was at a certain place, namely on the road to Damascus, that St. Paul saw the vision and heard the voice. It will also have relations of resemblance and non-resemblance. It will be in certain respects like, and in certain respects unlike, sensory or aesthetic experiences. It will also have causal relations, since causality is a universal condition of the time-order.[4] Thus it will be the case that the divine moment will have effects in the world. Thus the mystic influences men, founds religious orders, works in the world. It will also be the case that the divine moment will be capable of being produced by appropriate causes. These causes will constitute what in the different religions is called the "path" to salvation. In most religions, moral behavior, especially the behavior characteristic of love, is at least among the major causes. In some religions asceticism is recommended. In India all sorts of physical and spiritual exercises—including in the early stages special methods of breathing, and later, efforts of mental concentration and meditation and the effort to stop conceptual thinking—are among the means which are believed to lead up to the supreme experience. In Buddhism we have "the noble eightfold path," which includes both moral behavior and mystic contemplation. In Christianity and most other religions prayer is a chief means of achieving communion with God, which means the evocation of the divine moment within the worshipper.

The point here to be made, however, does not concern the particular causes which may lead to the evocation of the

[4] We may ignore as irrelevant the alleged non-causality of electrons. Even if electrons are not merely useful fictions, they are not part of the world of our experience. That world is macroscopic, and in it causality reigns. It is ridiculous to try, as some scientists would apparently have us do, to solve the problems of the moral and religious life by means of the alleged indeterminacy of the electron. We cannot solve these problems by remaining within the natural order and affirming that religious phenomena are exceptions to its laws. Kant long ago saw the shallowness of any such attempt. To solve our problems we have to turn from the temporal to the eternal order.

eternal moment. Some of them may seem to us appropriate
and some inappropriate. The point on which it is desirable
to fasten is that, if the divine moment is considered from the
outside, it will have natural causes of some kind, and if some
of them seem to us inappropriate, or even debasing to the
divine, they cannot in reality in any way affect, alter, or
diminish the divine character of the moment itself. In a sense
any natural causation must seem inappropriate. But we seem
to see in moral endeavor, in the life of love, in purity of
heart, means which appear to us proper and appropriate to
salvation, because we perceive in them some analogy to the
"holy" character of the moment itself. On the other hand,
breathing exercises are apt to seem—to the western mind—
out of keeping with, or at least irrelevant to, that holy character. The question is of some importance because it throws
light on the relations between science and religion. For the
temporal means to salvation, lying as they do in the chain
of causes and effects, belong to the natural order which is
the territory over which science reigns. But the divine moment itself, regarded as from within itself, belongs to the
sphere of religion.

Now this means that it is impossible for religion to dictate
to science, or in general to the conceptual intellect which is
concerned with the natural order, what can or what cannot
be causes of the divine moment. No doubt it is usually the
religious man who discovers these causes. It is he who finds
in his experience that prayer, or fasting, or the moral life,
bring him nearer to God. But in seeking and discovering
causes and effects he is acting as a natural man; he is within
the natural order, and is therefore himself a sort of scientist.
And it is at least conceivable that a scientist of the ordinary
sort might make discoveries which would have a bearing on
the causation of religious states, and that these discoveries
might come as a shock to the religious man, and have some
tendency to undermine his faith—unless he is firm in his understanding that no causes of the religious moment, however

materialistic they may seem, can in the slightest degree detract from the divine character of the religious revelation itself. This is but an instance of the general truth that no conceivable scientific discovery could ever destroy religion, if it is true, as is here contended, that science and religion concern two wholly different orders of being, the temporal and the eternal.

Let us suppose that some scientific person should succeed in proving that there is a correlation between capacity for mystic experience and a glandular condition of the mystic's body. He might even show that the administration of a certain drug could produce a state of mystical illumination. The question to be asked is: what then? Would this shock us? Or ought it to shock us? Above all, would it destroy our faith by showing that mystic illumination is after all nothing but an illusory subjective state of consciousness?

The possible glandular causation of the religious consciousness ought in no way to disturb or alarm us. For in taking the external view of the divine moment we have handed ourselves over to the naturalistic view-point, which we must then loyally accept. The divine moment will be, in itself, what it is—divine, eternal, infinite, supreme, transcendent of all time, of all causes, of all earthy things— utterly unaffected by the time relations and the causal relations which it may have when it is viewed externally as a moment within the natural order. Moreover the correlation of spiritual vision with a condition of the glands would be no more than an instance of the fact that, in general, mind and body are inter-related. If it is shocking to ask whether a man without a certain gland could achieve communion with God, why would it not be shocking to ask whether a man with a portion of his brain cut out could achieve such communion? It is reasonable to suppose that a state of mind is always correlated with a state of the brain. Presumably, then, the physical brain of the great mystic differs in some way from the physical brain of the non-mystic. Why then should not their glands also differ? And if so, it would be the case that the state of the glands of the mystic would appear as in the natural order a causal condition of his illumination.

We have to learn that we should never seek to defend religious truth by making it an exception to the natural order. To do this is to degrade it by making it a part of the natural order, a thing or fact which, though in the natural order, will not submit to the laws of the natural order. All history shows that this way of defending the things of the spirit always ends in defeat. And the long sad history of the defeats inflicted by science on religion have been due to nothing else than the false conception of religion as being concerned with facts in the natural order. God is not a fact, a thing, an object, or an existence. To consider Him one is to invite disaster. For "fact," "thing," "object," and "existence" are words or concepts taken from the vocabulary of the language of the natural order, and they apply only to the natural order. To be a fact means to be in systematic relations with other facts, and to be in such relations is to be finite and to belong to the order of time. "Fact," "existence," and the rest, if applied to God, are metaphors. It is true that the eternal moment, if it is considered externally, is then a fact, a part of the stream of time. But in itself it is not a fact.

CHAPTER 6 RELIGIOUS SYMBOLISM

RELIGIOUS SYMBOLISM DIFFERS FROM ALL NON-RELIGIOUS symbolism in two respects. In the first place, the symbolical propositions of religion cannot be translated into literal propositions, whereas all non-religious symbolic propositions—provided their symbolism is legitimate and not mere metaphor—can be so translated. The translation of religious symbolism into literal language is rendered impossible by the ineffability of religious experience. What the religious symbolic proposition stands for is not a literal proposition but an experience. In the second place, whereas in non-religious symbolism the relation between the symbol and the symbolizandum is that of "meaning," in religious symbolism the relation is that of evocation. Although we have so far spoken of the religious language "meaning" the experience, this is not the most accurate account. The symbol does not mean, but evokes, the experience. For a meaning is, in strictness, a concept; whereas here there is no concept. Thus when Plotinus speaks of "the flight of the alone to the Alone," and the positivist or the empiricist asserts that these words are meaningless, he is right. Yet this does not import that the words are nonsense locutions, mere senseless noises which a man makes like a cough or a sneeze—though it is possible that this is what the positivist intends. If this were so, it would be impossible to explain why generations of men have quoted those famous words. The explanation is that the words evoke in us a measure of the same experience which the author of them had. Our experience may be but a dim reflection of what was in him bright and clear. Our spirits vibrate faintly in unison with the soul of the great mystic, as a tuning fork vibrates faintly in response to the sound of the clear bell. But it is our own spontaneous experience which is evoked; it is not his experience which is communicated to us. His words are as grappling irons let down into the depths of our subconsciousness, which draw our own inner experiences nearer to the conscious threshold. But they are not, for most of us, drawn above the threshold. They remain below the surface faintly visible. Therefore they appear at the upper levels of our consciousness as faint hints, glimpses, and sometimes as mere vague feelings.

If it be asked *how* religious language evokes mystic experience in us, the question can no more be answered than the question how music—those meaningless sounds—evokes in us the feelings, the moods, the emotions which it does evoke. All we can say, in both cases, is simply that this is what happens. For the matter of that, as Hume showed, this is all that can be said in any case of cause and effect. We cannot even say how heat causes the particles of that which is heated to travel at higher speeds. We cannot say how heat causes water to boil. We can only say that it does so. There is therefore nothing out of the common in the causal relation of evocation.

If no concept of the divine is possible, and yet the structure of our minds is such that we are compelled to think in concepts if we think at all, it follows inevitably that, in thinking of the divine, we shall apply to it concepts which do not fit it. It is for this reason that all propositions about the divine are false. But if this is so, why do we employ one concept rather than another? Why is God love rather than hate? Why righteousness rather than unrighteousness? Where all is falsehood, what does it matter which falsehood we utter?

It is commonly said that although religious language, if taken literally, is false, yet one symbol is more "adequate" than another. Thus Dean Inge writes: "it is true that all our language about God must be inadequate and symbolic; but that is no reason for discarding all symbols, as if we could in that way know God as He knows Himself." [1]

But if God is not love, pity, power, in a literal sense, in what sense is He these things? And if these concepts taken

[1] *Christian Mysticism*, p. 111.

literally are false, how can they be less false than any other symbols which we might hit upon merely by chance? We use such phrases as more or less "adequate." But what does "adequate" mean? How can that which is false be nevertheless in some degree adequate? It is natural to explain this by saying that the symbol possesses some truth and some untruth. Then the one which contains more truth and less untruth will be the more adequate. Thus to call an ellipse a circle would at least be nearer the truth than to call it a square. For to call it a circle contains an element of truth, namely that it is a curve and not a construction of straight lines. But if this account of what "adequate" means is applied to religious symbolism, it will imply that the more adequate symbol, which we apply to God, is analyzable into conceptual parts, and that, among the sub-concepts so obtained by analysis, some are quite true of God, although others are false; just as the sub-concept "curved," which can be abstracted by analysis from "circle," is quite true of the circle. On this account, therefore, there exist concepts, of which the human mind is capable, which are perfectly true of God. But this amounts to saying that God is, after all, conceptually intelligible in some degree, that He can be apprehended, at least in some degree, by concepts. But this conflicts with the negative divine, and with the mystery and incomprehensibility of God. It means that His mystery and incomprehensibility are mere rhetorical exaggerations. And these conclusions we cannot accept.

Evidently we shall have to investigate further the conceptions of the adequate and inadequate. While we feel that they must have some meaning, we do not yet understand what they mean; and we must assert that theologians have so far used them without understanding them, and without any attempt to give a proper analysis of them.

One of the best writers on the relation of the religious symbol to the symbolizandum is Rudolph Otto,[2] and al-

[2] *The Idea of the Holy.*

though we shall find it impossible to accept his account, there is much to be learned from it, and we will make it the starting point of our discussion. Otto says that the numinous, which is his name for the pure religious experience, is felt as being ineffable and incapable of conceptualization. Nevertheless the mystic sees some analogy between a non-natural character of the numen and some natural quality of things which he has experienced in the ordinary world. He seizes upon the natural quality and uses it as a metaphor or "ideogram" for the non-natural character of the numen. This is the way in which religious symbolism arises, and this is the nature of religious symbolism. For instance, one aspect of the numinous is that it possesses a character which is perhaps best described as "awfulness," in the sense of producing religious awe. Words like "dread" and "fear" may also be used, but "awe" is the best word. Not one of these words, however, not even "awe," actually describes the numinous feeling. They are all ordinary natural concepts, derived from natural things, which can never therefore really express the nature of the numinous. Nevertheless there is some analogy, some resemblance, between natural dread or awe and the numinous feeling. Therefore "dread" and "awe" are used as metaphors or ideograms of it. Thus arise such expressions as "the fear of God," "the wrath of God"; and from thence, when these expressions are taken literally, come such intellectual propositions and beliefs as that God can be angry or jealous.

To give another instance, the numinous, besides having the character symbolized as awfulness, has another non-natural character which Otto calls "fascination." This attractive character of the numen, which is in contrast to the repellent character of awfulness, is of course indescribable by any natural concept. But the mystic sees an analogy between it and the natural qualities of love, graciousness, and so on. Grace and love then become symbols for the supernatural character which they only metaphorically describe.

So also "power," "pity," "knowledge," and presumably also "mind"—although Otto does not give this last as an example —are ideograms for the characters of the numinous, which they do not really describe but only symbolically shadow forth. Thus we get such intellectual propositions as "God is love," "God is a mind, a person," and so on.

The great psychological insight of Otto's account, and its suggestiveness for religious thinking, cannot be denied. Nevertheless the relation between the symbol and the numen cannot be what he implies. The relation implied is that of likeness or resemblance. The natural feeling of love is something *like* the directly apprehended character of the numen, although there is also a relation of unlikeness. The resemblance is only partial, but it is real. Presumably on this account a more adequate symbol will be one which bears more resemblance to the symbolizandum, while a less adequate symbol will be one which bears less. And presumably some symbols, hate for instance, would be wholly unlike the symbolizandum and therefore not merely inadequate, but wholly false.

This is a natural view to take because it agrees with the general character of symbolism in spheres other than the religious. In general the relation of symbol to symbolizandum is that of resemblance. The sensuous metaphor bears in some way a likeness to that of which it is a metaphor. The troubles of which Hamlet speaks are like the sea in being multitudinous, as the waves of the sea are mutitudinous, in being alarming, overwhelming, difficult to cope with, and so on. The journey of Bunyan's pilgrim bears a resemblance to the life-journey of the Christian. The simile in poetry is in some way like the situation or thing of which it is a simile.

But no view of this kind fits the special case of religious symbolism. For if there is a resemblance between the natural character which is used as a symbol and the supernatural reality which it symbolizes, then there is a common element as between the two, and therefore the possibility of a concept. For to have a concept of something only means to apprehend a resemblance or common element as between it and other things which we, because of the resemblance, place in the same class.

We must therefore seek some other account of religious symbolism, and of the meaning of the terms adequacy and inadequacy.

Let us return to the image of the intersection of the natural order by the divine order in that moment which is internally eternal, but externally a moment in time. This moment lies transparent, lucent, brightly lighted, fully self-conscious, self-aware, in the spirit of the great mystic. In other men it exists below the level of the threshold of consciousness, veiled, dim, misty, even altogether dark. If we are to conceive, as we surely must, that the intersection of the divine and the natural occurs not only at every moment of time in the life-history of every man, but also throughout the universe at every space-time point of the natural order—so that there is no part of the world which is wholly abandoned of God—we must carry our conception further down to the lower levels of the scale of being. The divine moment must exist, though far more deeply buried, in the life of the animal, the plant, and even in the life of the metal and the rock.

In this way we arrive at the conception of a scale of being, an order of natural existences, rank above rank. At the bottom we shall have what we ordinarily call dead matter, above it plants, then animals, then men, and finally those supermen whom we call mystics. What makes an existence higher or lower in this scale will be the degree in which the divine moment is realized in it, the depth to which, in its mentality, that moment is sunk in its sub-conscious, or the height to which it is raised, near to the bright light of consciousness, or above the threshold. In the mystic it is fully conscious. In the ordinary man it is usually below the threshold but can be brought, by evocation, so near the surface that he

becomes dimly aware of it. But there are levels below levels
of the unconscious, depths below depths. In the animal it is
sunk deeper, so that it cannot be evoked at all, cannot by
any means be dragged up from the depths. In the life of the
plant nothing at all can be evoked, not even—we commonly
suppose—a conscious awareness of physical objects, the sun,
the wind, the cool of the night, the light of the day. In the
animal these at least have been drawn upward to the level
of conscious awareness, but in the plant nothing. Its life,
from the first day to the last, is an unbroken hypnotic sleep
wherein it responds to stimuli blindly, without being aware
of them, which is also the case with the hypnotized or som-
nambulist human being. And we must surmise that, in the
metal or the rock, the consciousness, which is its life and its
being, exists only in an utter blackness which we may try
faintly to understand through analogies with our own experiences of sleep, hypnosis, or somnambulism. In that utter
darkness, in that blackness beyond all blackness, which is
not to be plumbed by any human device, must lie the eternal
moment, buried and imprisoned, perhaps to be released into
the light in some inconceivably far off future epoch of the
world.

We may conceive this scale of being also as a process of
the self-realization of God. He is present in the experience
of the mystic, and is there fully at one with Himself, self-
identical, completely self-realized, completely manifest. At
that moment there is no otherness as between God and the
world. For the division of subject and object, which is here
abolished, is identical with the division of God from the
world. The otherness of the world from God is the basis
and foundation and original meaning of the subject-object
structure of experience. Thus in the mystic moment subject
and object, God and the world, the divine order and the
natural order, have coalesced, become one in the division-
less, relationless, ultimate unity of things. God has come to
Himself. God is totally God.

In the common man the divine has also realized itself, but less fully. And this is the same as saying that the eternal moment in him lies normally below the level of his conscious life, in the twilight of his mind, not yet self-conscious, self-realized. And we continue the regress downward into the lower orders of existence. In what we call wholly inanimate beings, where the twilight has given place to the blackness of the pit, God, though not absent, is lost, self-estranged, furthest away from His complete self-being. It may be that the notion of the descent of God into hell is a faint unconscious symbolization of this.

We can now interpret the nature of religious symbolism, and especially the meaning of the terms "more adequate" and "less adequate." The relation between the symbol and the symbolizandum is not that of resemblance, but that of greater or less *nearness* to the full self-realization of God. Certainly "near" and "far" are metaphors, but it is easy to interpret them. In the scale of being, one level is nearer to God's self-realization than a second if between it and that full self-realization there intervene fewer levels of being than between the second and that full self-realization.

This can be applied to the understanding of the relative adequacy or inadequacy of religious symbols in the following way. The more adequate symbols are those which are taken from the highest ranks of existence; the less adequate are those which are taken from lower ranks. Hence "mind" or "personality" are the general symbols which are most adequate to God, while symbols taken from the level of inanimate existence, such as physical forces and lumps of matter, will be the least adequate. Thus it is truer to say that God is a mind or a person than that He is a force. For the word force refers primarily to such existences as gravitation, cohesion, and the like, which belong to the lowest order of beings, those furthest away from the divine self-realization. It is true that the notion of power is not thought of as a wholly inadequate symbol for God, and that being all-powerful is conceived as one of His main attributes. And it may be supposed that power and force are the same thing. This is to some extent merely a matter of words. Power and even force are concepts taken from more than one level of existence, and to this extent the words are ambiguous. Gravitation is a typical example of a purely physical force. But of course we also speak of a powerful mind and a forceful personality. Hence to attribute power to God, in the sense of physical power or force, would be recognized at once as an extremely crude and inadequate symbol. But to attribute power to Him, in the sense in which minds and personalities are powerful, is not inadequate symbolism.

In the scale of being "life" comes half-way between dead matter and mind. Life, but not mind, belongs to plants. Therefore "life" is a less adequate symbol for God than mind or personality, but a more adequate symbol than such as are taken from the world of dead matter. We have yet to discuss the ethical symbolism which attributes love and goodness to God. But we may note at once that it takes its symbols from the level of mind, and is therefore more adequate than a symbolism based upon the lower level of life. In other words, it is truer and more adequate to say that God is love than that God is life. The "living God" is indeed an important and valuable symbol. But we have a situation here similar to that which we noticed in the case of the symbol of force or power. In the most general terms the cosmic order, whose lowest term is dead matter, passes upward through the successive levels of plant life, animal life, consciousness, mind and personality. Thus life belongs specifically to the comparatively low level of the plant kingdom. Considered in this way it is a very inadequate symbol for God. But life stretches upward from the plant stratum, through that of the animal, to that of mind. Animals and men are also living. Hence the word "living," as applied to

God, must be thought of as an attribute of persons, not of plants. And considered in this way it is not, of course, an inadequate symbol.

We noted that symbols taken from the world of dead matter and force are the most inadequate. And if we should suggest that God is a material being, a lump of clay, or even an electric force, we should feel at once the utter inadequacy and inappropriateness of the symbolism. Even here, however, we should not have total untruth. This kind of symbolism is the source of what we call idolatry, the worship of wood and stone, of the sun and moon. In idolatry the higher symbolism of life and mind is not absent, since the stone or wood are fashioned in the images of living beings, and the heavenly bodies are conceived as animated by spiritual presences. Idolatry is thus not to be thought of as wholly false religion, the work of the devil, but as an evolutionary level of religion in which only the most inadequate symbols are applied to the divine.

The types of symbol which we have so far considered, power, force, life, mind, personality, have not as such any ethical content. These types are based upon an order of being which proceeds from lower to higher. But the "lower" and "higher" are not ethically lower and higher. Their order is an order of being, not an order of value; a cosmic or ontological order, not an axiological order. In other words, although mind is higher in the scale of being than plant life, this does not mean that it is in itself ethically better. We apply to God value words such as good, righteous, loving, gracious. But mind, personality, and life, are not value words. They are ethically neutral.

This statement is likely to be doubted. We are accustomed to think of mind as something higher than life, and of life as something higher than dead matter. This idea of an order of being is rooted in our instinctive consciousness, and has been reinforced by evolutionary theories. We naturally associate the terms higher and lower with the ethical words better and worse, and suppose that they mean the same thing. Moreover in this instinctive identification of the cosmically higher with the ethically higher we are in the end right. I shall show that the order of value runs in fact parallel to the order of being, and that what is higher in the one scale is also higher in the other. Nevertheless the two scales are not the same. Mind and life do not necessarily and in themselves import any kind of moral goodness. A plant is not as such more "virtuous" than a stone, nor a mind than a plant. A mind is not necessarily good. It may indeed be almost wholly evil. The devil, after all, is a mind and a personality.

It is common knowledge that the biological theory of evolution contains as such no value implications. There is not the slightest reason, within science, for identifying the evolutionary process with an ethical advance. That process has been described as a change from the less complex to the more complex, or from the less organized and integrated to the more organized and integrated. And there is no ground for identifying the more or less complex and integrated, as such, with more or less valuable. To see in biological evolution an ethical progress is therefore commonly recognized as a naïve error. Nevertheless this so-called vulgar error cannot but be founded on a true intuition. The order of being must in reality be an order of values. But to show this requires a new effort of thought, a new analysis.

What is required is to establish, first, that there is in the universe an order of values as well as an order of being; and secondly, that what is lower in the one scale is also lower in the other scale, and that what is higher in the one is also higher in the other. It is necessary to do this in order to justify the application of value symbolism to God. What we have so far shown is only that predicates taken from the level of mind and personality are more adequate symbols for God than predicates taken from the lower levels of life or material forces. But there are large numbers of value predicates which we apply symbolically to God, but which are not justified by this procedure. God is good, righteous, just, merciful, loving, compassionate. What, we must now ask, is the justification of these predicates? In especial, why is one value predicate more true or adequate than another? Why is it appropriate to say that God is love, and inappropriate to say that He is hate? Why is He righteous rather than unrighteous? We have seen only that mind is a relatively adequate symbol for God. But a mind is not necessarily a good mind, nor is it necessarily a loving mind. Hate, just as much as love, is a quality which belongs to the level of mind. The value symbolism which we apply to God is not justified by the idea of a cosmic scale of being, because that scale is not a scale of values.

No doubt we shall find that what, in the value order, is more valuable, is nearer to God than what is less valuable, just as in the cosmic order we found that what is cosmically higher is nearer to the divine than what is cosmically lower. But this will be the case only if God Himself can be conceived in value terms as the supremely excellent. And the question we have to ask is: what ground have we for so conceiving Him?

The answer can be found in the eternal moment only as viewed from the inside. If we look only at the natural order we do not find a scale of values. One thing in it is as good as another thing; or rather, all things are equally indifferent. The natural order, viewed simply as natural, is not a moral order. We can, of course, call good those things which please us, and bad those things which displease us. And this, or some version of this, is in fact the naturalistic account of values. But this is plainly subjectivistic. Values are then dependent on the human mind, its desires and purposes. Good and evil are defined in terms of human happiness or pleasures. This is not false. The naturalistic solution of a philosophical problem is a true solution. It is a true statement about the natural order. The natural order *is* devoid of values. Taken by itself, there is no one thing in the natural order that is better than any other thing, except in the sense of being more pleasing to human beings. Thus if there were no human beings in the world—if, for example, the human race were wiped out tomorrow—there would be no values in the universe. This is often expressed by saying that the universe is indifferent to values, that it cares nothing about good or evil, that values are only human. It is for this reason also that science has nothing to say about values. It is merely descriptive of the *facts* of the universe. For the sphere of science is the natural order, its facts and its laws. And science cannot say anything about values, because values are not found in the natural order.

To find the scale of values then we have to look to the divine order, that is to say, to the eternal moment as viewed from within. And this means that we have to look to the experience of the mystic. There we find the answer to our problem lying immediately to our hand. For we find therein, not indeed the entire scale of values, but only its highest term, its apex, its supreme value. For all who have dwelt self-consciously in the eternal moment, in the full light of its explicit self-realization, who have thus met the Eternal face to face, are agreed that, whatever else it is, it is the experience of a supreme and transcendent value. The words used are many. It is the experience of a supreme blessedness. It is bliss unspeakable. God, thus immediately experienced, is love and peace. He is the great light. He is the blessed calm, the refuge, the goal. He is the good, the righteous. And those who have thus fully entered into that experience feel themselves as enveloped, overwhelmed, swallowed up, as in a vast ocean of love and peace and goodness and ineffable bliss. Since the experience is ineffable, these words, love, bliss, peace, calm, must themselves be no more than metaphors. They are taken from the ordinary vocabulary of natural modes of happiness. But we must suppose that they are the most adequate of all ethical symbols, and this must mean that they are "nearer" to the divine nature than any other symbols would be.

It is interesting to note that although the mystic in general uses common words, natural concepts, as symbols of the divine, yet occasionally he either coins a new word to describe his unique experience, or at least uses an old natural word in an especial mystical sense. This is the case, for example, with the word "blessedness." Blessedness is not at all the same as happiness, though happiness is its naturalistic counterpart. The religious man does not seek happiness; he seeks blessedness. Whatever may be the root and derivation of this word in common language, it is now a wholly religious and mystical word, and not a part of the common naturalistic vocabulary at all. There can be a great deal of happiness in the world, that is, in the natural order. But there is no blessedness whatever. Whoever in any degree knows blessedness, whoever even understands the meaning of the word, derives that knowledge and that understanding from the influence of the divine moment within himself, even though it be far sunk in his unconscious life.

Thus the highest point, the apex, of the scale of values is fixed. Its justification is in direct experience. What about the lower levels of the scale? That they are not found directly within the eternal moment, as in the highest level, simply means that God in Himself is only the supreme value. He is not any lower values. Yet we may surmise that lower values scale down from the supreme value, just as lower levels of being scale down from the supreme level of being. And since the highest value is now fixed, we may suppose that the lower and lower levels will be those which are further and further away from the highest, precisely as was the case in the order of being. Dead matter was the furthest from God in the scale of being. We may therefore believe that it is also the furthest away in the order of values. And above it, in order of value, will come life and then mind.

Is there any justification for this suggestion other than a possible analogy between the two orders? Now if we are to find any justification, we are not likely to find it in the workings of the conceptual intellect. For the conceptual intellect is the mode of consciousness which apprehends the natural order, and in the natural order there is no scale of values. The mode of consciousness which apprehends the divine order is intuition, and it is in intuition therefore that we may expect to find indications of the scale of values. We find such an indication, in the first place, in the intuitive belief, to which we have already referred, that biological evolution is in some sense an ethical advance. Every one knows that the evolutionary process has back-tracked and wandered into blind alleys. Yet the over-all picture appears to be an advance. And however much we are told that the more complex is not as such the more ethical, and that the reading of value judgments into biology is a vulgar error, the human mind persists in its intuitive conviction that what is higher in the evolutionary scale is also higher in the scale of values. It is a fact that evolution has proceeded from protoplasm to man through intermediate ranks of living beings. It is an ineradicable intuition that a man is a higher being than a horse or a crocodile, not merely in the sense of being more complex and differentiated, but in a value sense as well. We may be told that this is merely human conceit, that by "better" and "higher" all we mean is "more like us," and that the crocodile's opinion might well be the opposite of ours. Dominated and bedevilled as we are by scientific modes of thinking, we may well come to believe these statements and to disbelieve in our own intuitions. But we certainly have the intuitions; and to suppose that they indicate a true aspect of reality is just as good a hypothesis for explaining them as is the supposition that they are merely due to our self-conceit.

There is however another intuition which provides evidence of our contention. The moral intuitions of civilized mankind are unanimous that among human modes of seeking satisfaction—what the hedonist calls "pleasures"—there is a scale of higher and lower. No doubt this intuitive scale is exceedingly vague. But it is none the less real and exerts a strong influence on life. In general, intellectual, aesthetic, and moral satisfactions are thought to be higher, that is, more valuable, than the pleasures and satisfactions of the senses. The activities and pleasures of which a man is capable are more noble than the activities and pleasures of a pig. There may be nothing wrong with the pleasures of eating, drinking, and sex. They have their proper place in life. To think them intrinsically evil is an error. But they are inferior. To use an example of Plato's, there is pleasure to be obtained from scratching one's skin where it itches. Presumably there is nothing wicked in doing so. Why should not a man enjoy this pleasure? Yet it cannot be thought to be *equal*, in a value sense, with the satisfaction to be obtained from hearing great music or poetry, nor even with the intellectual satisfaction which the mathematician presumably obtains from his intellectual activities.

Every student of philosophy knows that the problem of how this conception of higher and lower pleasures is to be explained or justified is fraught with difficulty. Plato, Bentham, Mill, and many others have discussed it and suggested various theories. But for the moment I wish to insist upon three points. First, it is an intuition, not a result of any reasoned process. Second, it is an intuition universal, or nearly universal, among civilized races; it is not the idiosyncrasy of some regional culture. Third, the fact that it has puzzled philosophers for two thousand years, has presented to them in fact a knot which they have not been able to untie, is due to their having looked for a solution of the problem always and only in the natural order; whereas it can be understood only as an influx of the divine order into the natural order, an effect of the eternal moment upon history and the moments of time.

First, it is an intuition. This, I think, requires little proof. It is the sort of thing of which we are apt to say that we believe it—if we do believe it—"instinctively." The word instinct has here no scientific connotations. It does not matter what our theory about "instincts" may be. It does not matter even if we doubt that any such psychological states or factors exist. Everyone knows what is meant by such a phrase as "I felt instinctively that. . . ." It means that the belief or feeling appeared in our consciousness immediately, and not as a result of any conscious reasoned process. It is true that some intuitive or instinctive beliefs may be explained as due to unconscious inference. This is a very obscure subject. Perhaps one ought to distinguish between genuine intuitions, such as those which are the basis of the religious consciousness, and quasi-intuitions, which are really unconscious inferences. It cannot be denied, however, that the belief in higher and lower satisfactions is in some sense intuitive. The mere fact that it presents a problem to the philosophers proves this. For their problem is precisely to give a rational account of it, to show on what reasons, if any, it is based. Their trouble is that they have not been able to find the reasons. It cannot therefore have been based on a reasoning process among common men.

Secondly, the intuition is common to most civilized races. This could be documented at great length and with elaborate erudition. It will be sufficient here to point out the following facts. The intuition appears in one form or another in the ancient Greco-Roman world, in Christian culture, and in Hinduism and Buddhism. And it can hardly be doubted that a student of Chinese and Japanese religious and moral literature would be able to point to its presence there. In the ancient world it is the essence of the Socratic doctrine of the soul, and of the Socratic conviction that the things of the soul are more noble than the things of the body. It permeates Plato's dialogues. "Reason," according to the *Republic*, is of an intrinsically higher nature than the emotions and the sensuous appetites, and is therefore their natural ruler. The word "reason" is, of course, very ambiguous, nor does Plato define it. But it is evident that he means the "higher" faculties of the intellect as opposed to the "lower" faculties of the senses. The Platonic "forms" or "ideas," around which Plato throws a halo of mystical feeling, and which represent the divine, or semi-divine, element in the world, are known by the eye of reason and not by the eye of the body. Likewise in Christian thought bodily satisfaction has always been regarded as on a lower level than those satisfactions which are connected with the faculties of the soul and mind. Exactly the same thing is true of Hindu and Buddhist thought. The exaggeration of this tendency is asceticism, which may be defined as the belief that the pleasures of the body are not merely inferior, but positively evil. Asceticism has no part in the best Greek thought, and was positively repudiated by the Buddha, who preached a doctrine of "the middle way" as between sensual indulgence and asceticism. It has appeared at various times in the history of Christian monasticism. But its occasional presence in all the great religions is evidence of the universal force of the intuition which we are discussing, since it consists in nothing but an over-emphasis on that intuition.

It may be useful to give an example from a modern writer on ethics. Regarding the assumption that two pleasures which are equal in quantity (intensity, duration, etc.) must therefore be equal in value, and that one cannot be intrinsically better or higher than the other, Professor G. E. Moore writes: "It"—i.e. this assumption—"involves our saying that, for instance, the state of mind of a drunkard, when he is intensely pleased with breaking crockery, is just as valuable, in itself—just as well worth having, as that of a man who is fully realizing all that is exquisite in the tragedy of King Lear, provided only the mere quantity of pleasure in both cases is the same." Professor Moore rejects this view and proceeds: "of course, here again, the question is *quite incapable of proof* either way. And if anybody . . . does come to the conclusion that no kind of enjoyment is ever intrinsically better than another . . . *there is no way of proving* that he is wrong. But it seems to me almost impossible that anybody, who does really get the question clear, should take such a view; and, if anybody were to, I think it is *self-evident* that he would be wrong." [3]

It is evident that the moral conviction to which Professor Moore refers is identical with the belief, which we are discussing, that the things of the soul and mind are intrinsically more noble than the things of the body. And the words which I have italicized make plain that the conviction is an intuition, and not a reasoned belief—although, of course, Professor Moore does not mean to commit himself to any theory of intuition, and does not in fact use that word.

The evidence here quoted seems to show beyond doubt that the intuition is not a peculiarity of any one culture, but is practically universal among civilized races of men. It is not confined to Christian thought, for it is found in the ancient pagan world. It is not confined to the West, for it appears equally strongly in India.

Our third point is that this intuition is in reality an influx from the divine moment into the natural world. We have seen that, although the two orders are wholly separate, yet the eternal moment, considered externally as a moment of time, has both causes and effects in the natural order. There is therefore an inflow of feelings from it into the natural order. This takes place in two ways. In the first place, the great mystic carries over into time the aura of his vision, producing moral and religious effects in the world. He influences other men. In the second place—and this is the more important point—the divine moment within the subconsciousness of the ordinary "non-mystic" projects influences into the upper levels of his conscious life, which appear there in the form of vague feelings. These include his moral intuitions, of which one is that the things of the mind and soul are nobler than the things of the body.

[3] G. E. Moore, *Ethics*, p. 237. Italics mine.

But we have failed to show so far *why*, even within the divine order, mind is higher, in a value sense, than matter. We have shown that the divine moment in itself is the supreme value, the highest point of the scale of values. But we have not justified any order of values below this supreme point. How is this to be done? The answer is that our moral intuition gives evidence that the order of being and the order of values are the same. The order of being, proceeding from the lower to the higher levels, is: dead matter, life, mind, mystical consciousness. In this order, matter, which means in general the things of the body and the senses, comes at the bottom of the scale. Above it come life and mind; and at the top the divine moment. But this is also the moral order as evidenced by the intuitive moral consciousness. The reason therefore, *why* the things of the body are morally lower than the things of the mind, is that mind is "nearer" to the supreme value of the full self-realization of God than matter is.

This truth is discoverable only by religious and moral intuition, by taking account, that is to say, of the divine order as well as of the natural order. Therefore any philosophy which is based wholly on the evidences of the natural order finds extreme difficulty in justifying our moral intuitions. This is the reason why philosophers have generally found the problem insoluble. They have tried to give a purely naturalistic account of it. This is the reason why J. S. Mill found himself in trouble on the question of higher and lower pleasures. He insisted on the hedonistic view that pleasure is the sole criterion of all value, but equally insisted that the pleasures of the mind are intrinsically higher than the pleasures of the body. His critics had no difficulty in showing that these two views, both of which he held, are inconsistent with one another. For to assert that of two pleasures which are equal in quantity, one is nevertheless better than the other, implies some standard of value other than pleasure.

If all other things are to be judged by the standard of pleasure, by what standard are pleasures themselves to be judged? It must plainly be by some standard other than pleasure. This famous dispute is at least evidence of Mill's high honesty. In his insistence that, whatever his own hedonistic theory might demand, bodily pleasures are in fact of lower quality than intellectual pleasures, he was relying upon his own deep moral intuitions rather than on his theory.

The naturalist can, indeed, give his own account of the matter. He may take either of two courses. He may base his theory frankly and explicitly upon intuitions. And many ethical philosophers have done this. But in that case, assuming that he gives no recognition to the divine order, but bases his entire philosophy upon naturalistic considerations, the intuition will appear in his theory as no more than an unaccountable brute fact of human consciousness. It just is the case that human minds have a psychological twist such that one pleasure appears to them better than another, notwithstanding that both are equal in quantity.

Other naturalistic philosophers will attempt to explain the intuition as the result of unconscious inductive inference based upon ages of human experience. It has been found over long ages that in fact the things of the mind yield in the long run more happiness to men than the things of the body. For this reason they have come to be called "higher." And purely natural reasons can be given why intellectual things yield more happiness. They are, for instance, rarely anti-social, whereas the pleasures of the body, if over-indulged, especially those of sex, often are so. A passion for art or mathematics usually hurts no one. But sexual passion, unless very carefully controlled, often produces disaster. The view that the moral intuition is the result of unconscious inductive inference, based on long human experience of the art of trying to live successfully and happily, has been urged by the present writer in earlier writings.

Such a naturalistic view of morals is not false. In fact *some* naturalistic theory of ethics *must* be true. For the two orders, the divine and the natural, are each self-contained. And because the natural order is self-contained, every natural fact must be capable of a complete explanation in naturalistic terms only. And the moral intuitions of man, as they appear in the time-order, are natural facts. So, for that matter, are his religious intuitions. The eternal moment, if viewed from the outside, is, as we have seen, a moment in time, a part of the natural order, involved in the universal network of causes and effects, and wholly explicable thereby. The same will of course be true of moral intuitions. It is true that the moral intuition, viewed naturalistically, will appear as a mere brute fact. But so will all other facts. This was the great insight of David Hume. If it is a mere brute fact that such and such a moral intuition appears in the human consciousness, it is equally a mere brute fact that heat boils water. That the natural order is self-contained is also the basis of the maxim of science that for every natural fact a natural cause must be found, and that appeal must never be made to supernatural intervention. The religious scientist often appears as an odd phenomenon. For, on the one hand, it is part of his creed that to bring in God to explain a particular phenomenon is unscientific, while on the other hand he is allowed to believe that in some way the universe as a whole—in distinction from any particular part of it, or any particular event within it—is the work of God.[4] This appears as a

---

[4] This is the most favorable account of the scientific-religious mind which can be given. It is probable, however, that many scientists, falling below this level, hold that the maxim of an orderly nature holds true in general, but allow themselves to imagine that there are, or have been, occasional exceptions in which God interferes. The last great scientist who openly took this view was, I believe, Newton, who supposed that the planets, if left to themselves, or rather to the law of gravitation, would deviate slightly from their proper paths, so that in the end they would fly off into space or approach nearer the sun—unless they were somehow prevented. God therefore occasionally pushed them back into their

perfectly arbitrary distinction, for which he can give no justification. Yet his instinct is right. It points to the wholly self-contained character of each of the two orders. If God is "wholly other" than the natural order, then also the natural order is "wholly other" than God. And this latter means that God is not a part of the natural order, and that all facts within that order must be capable of a completely naturalistic explanation. To give that explanation is the function of science. And the scientist who admits supernatural interventions and explanations is therefore being unscientific.

Nor would it be correct to say that, although a naturalistic theory of morals must be possible, it is nevertheless not the complete truth, but must be supplemented by the explanation here given of an influx of values from the eternal order into the temporal order. This influx is what we have insisted on. But it is not a "supplement" to the natural explanation. The latter is wholly complete in its own terms. The two explanations neither overlap, nor contradict one another, nor interfere with one another. Each stands wholly on its own ground, complete in itself. The naturalistic philosopher is just as right to pursue his kind of explanation of morals to the end, and to object to the intrusion into it of any supernaturalistic elements, as is the physical scientist to adopt the same attitude.

It is often asked whether values are absolute, eternal, and objective, or relative, temporal, and subjective. The answer is that they are both. There is an absolute scale of values, but it does not belong to the natural order. It is revealed only in

---

true places. Leibniz hinted that Newton's God was not only a mechanic, but a poor one at that, since He had to keep tinkering with His machine to make it go right. Nowadays any astronomer would officially profess to be scandalized by such a view as Newton's. But it is to be feared that unofficially, secretly, and furtively, many scientists suppose that there may be exceptional cases in which God intervenes—although fortunately these instances are always so far away, in time or space, that they do not interfere with the results of scientific experiments. Being human beings, they are likely to conceal these lapses from their colleagues, but especially from themselves.

the supreme moment of mystical illumination, or in those moral intuitions which are but lower powers or lesser degrees of that final illumination. But if we look at these value revelations from the outside, from that standpoint in which they appear as successive moments of time, they are then relative, temporal, and subjective. From that point of view, one thing is not "really" better than another thing, but is only so in so far as it achieves better our happiness or pleasure. And since the happiness of one man is not the same as the happiness of another, values will be relative. The most that one can then show will be that some values are more or less universal in the sense that there are some conditions of human happiness which are roughly the same for all normal men. Values viewed from the temporal standpoint will also be subjective. For the mystic illumination, viewed from the standpoint of time, is merely a subjective state of the mystic's mind, an illusion. It is only as viewed from within that it is a revelation of God. The scale of values which proceeds from the mystic illumination will also be, from the natural standpoint, a subjective illusion. God Himself will be an illusion. And these naturalistic conclusions are, from their own point of view, which is the temporal point of view, quite correct. For an illusion—whatever may be its precise epistemological definition—is certainly something which is contrary to fact. And God and eternity and the eternal order of values do not belong to the order of facts, which is the order of time. They belong to the eternal and the divine order.

Our attempt in this chapter has been to justify religious symbolism, to explain the relation of the symbol to the symbolizandum, and in particular to explain in what sense, and how, one religious symbol can be more adequate than another. We have found that there are two kinds of predicates which are symbolically applied to God. The first kind are ethically neutral, such as "mind," "person," "power." The second kind are value predicates, such as love, pity, mercy, justice, righteousness. The former were justified by the concept of an order of being, the latter by an order of values. In both cases the more adequate symbol is that which is a metaphor taken from a higher level of the scale, a "higher" level meaning one which is "nearer" to God.

GOD IS THE TRUTH. HE IS ALSO THE SUPREME REALITY. WE have to inquire what these predicates, truth and reality, mean as applied to God. They are, of course, symbolical. But we have to ask in what way these symbols are appropriate.

The sense in which God is the Truth must not be confused with the wholly different sense in which propositions, whether scientific or religious, are true. Scientific propositions are, or are intended to be, literally true. Religious propositions are symbolically true. They may be said to possess more truth, or less, in so far as their symbolism is more adequate, or less. But when God is called the Truth, it is not anything of this sort that is meant. For truth, in the sense in which even a religious creed is true, is an attribute of propositions. But God is not a proposition, and cannot be true in any such sense. Nor does the Truth of God mean merely that religious propositions about God are symbolically true. Truth is evidently an attribute of God Himself. "I am the Truth" does not mean "some propositions about Me are true."

Truth, as applied to God, is a value term. If God is the Good, and the Beautiful, He is also the True. One might perhaps be justified in suggesting that there is no special meaning to the word truth here, that it merely stands as a symbol of value in general, that its attribution to God means much the same as do the attributions of goodness and beauty, namely that God is the apex of value, the supreme value. This may be, to some extent, correct. It cannot be denied that there is a certain vagueness in the religious consciousness, and in the religious use of language, and that to tie down religious words too precisely to exact meanings is a mistake. And no doubt the word "truth" as applied to God is often thus vague and emotive. Nevertheless, I believe that there is here a more precise and subtle nuance of meaning which it will be instructive to uncover.

There is a very close connection between the religious consciousness and the aesthetic consciousness. What the exact connection is it would be extremely difficult to say. It will not do to identify them. The religious and the aesthetic each have their own specific characters, which serve to distinguish them from one another. But in some sense it is certain that the artistic is often mystical. What is called "nature mysticism," as found, for example, in the poetry of Wordsworth, is in some way an apprehension of the mystical and religious through the beauty of nature. I shall make no attempt here to set forth a theory of the nature of the relation of the mystical to the artistic, and shall content myself with the vague statement that there is a close relationship.

Now we find that just as the religious consciousness attributes truth to its object, so also—at least in many cases—does the aesthetic consciousness. This is directly expressed in the phrase of Keats' "Beauty is Truth, Truth Beauty." Even in the sober prose of critics and aesthetic philosophers, it is often maintained that art possesses a kind of truth, and even that it is a form of knowledge. But this truth and this knowledge cannot be of a propositional kind. It cannot be the case that the words "truth" and "knowledge" are used here in the same sense—the literal sense of the words—in which it is said that propositions are true and convey knowledge. They are used in some symbolic sense. Of course, a work of art may contain or express truths of a literal kind. These may be moral truths about human life, or philosophical truths about the world. They may, moreover, be very important components of the work of art, constituting in large measure its "greatness." Nevertheless to suppose that this literal sense of truth is what is meant by "Beauty is Truth," or by the theory of art as knowledge, would be a shallow interpretation. Beauty is truth in some deeper sense than this. Certainly Keats, the least intellectual or philosophical of poets, meant nothing of this kind. For the "truth" of which he spoke could be found even in those forms of beauty in which there is no shadow of intellectual content, in a simple blend of colors, for instance, or in non-representational music. The truth which is beauty must therefore be, like the truth which is God, non-propositional. The study of the former may therefore throw light on the latter. What then is the nature of this aesthetic truth?

We ask the same question, I believe, when we inquire what is the nature of the phenomenon of poetic *shock*. Consider Wordsworth's lines:

> "Will no one tell me what she sings?
> Perhaps the plaintive numbers flow
> For old unhappy far off things
> And battles long ago."

The commonplace doggerel of the first two lines serves only to set off and enhance the gasping shock, the catch of the breath, which comes upon us in the last two lines. There is in them the sense of a sudden tearing aside of the veil which normally hides, from our common day-light consciousness, the racial memory of that "pre-conscious terror," of which another poet speaks. There is the foreground of life, the fields, the sun, the girl singing, of which we are fully aware. And there is the dim background of the pre-conscious terror buried in the depths below the threshold. Wordsworth's lines throw a sudden shaft of light down into this dark subconscious region. Hence there is a sense of *revelation*. And it is this revelation which is characteristic of poetic shock.

We may take another example:

> "stout Cortez when with eagle eyes
> He stared at the Pacific—and all his men
> Looked at each other with a wild surmise
> Silent upon a peak in Darien."

Here all the lines are poetic, not doggerel. But as in Wordsworth's poem the special sense of shock comes with the last two lines. There is a crescendo of shock. What is its source, and what its nature?

We may say, perhaps, that the words evoke a vivid image, clear-cut, with sharp outlines, of the men, their movement suddenly arrested, stopped in mid-passage, standing rooted to the spot, silent, motionless. A fleeting instant of time, stopped in its flow, caught and held thus, frozen before our gaze. But why should this produce in us the effect it does, the thrill, the fascination? I think it is because we see in this frozen moment of time, standing for ever still, an image and symbol of eternity. Time has become timeless. And the timeless, the motionless, the silent, are symbols of the eternal.

If this analysis is correct, this passage of Keats is more definitely mystical than are Wordsworth's lines. For they act as a revelation, or suggestion, of the eternal order, whereas Wordsworth's poem reveals only an element of our sub-consciousness—the pre-conscious terror—which is not in itself religious, but has to do with events in the temporal order. But what is characteristic of both is their revelatory character. This, as we see from the example of Wordsworth's poem, is not necessarily a revelation of the divine order.[1] The revelation consists in the sudden and unexpected exposure to light of elements normally buried in the subconscious darkness.

What I have called poetic shock is not, of course, peculiar to poetry, much less to some selected set of poems such as those from which I have quoted. All art is shock. I have merely selected some lines of poetry in which the phenomenon of shock is perhaps at a maximum, so that its characteristics are easily discerned.

Now the same character of revelation, which we find in poetry, attaches to mystical illumination, although here the

[1] Hence what is here said must not be confused with what is commonly called "the revelatory theory of art."

revelation is always of the divine. The eternal moment lies normally in the subconscious. Mystical illumination consists in its sudden appearance in full light above the threshold. Moreover there is a further likeness between the aesthetic and the religious. The language both of art and of religion is evocative, not scientific or informative. It does not give information about any object outside us. It evokes what is within. It draws to the light what lies below the threshold. This is true of music as well as of poetry. The music evokes the hidden mood or feeling.

In what sense, then, do we have truth, whether in the artistic or the religious sphere? Truth, I suggest, means the sense or feeling of revelation. But here there is a danger of mistake. Both the words truth and revelation are likely to suggest to us that what is revealed is some true proposition. We have to avoid this error. What is revealed—in the religious case at any rate—is God, not a proposition about God. And that God is the Truth means that He is the content of revelation.

Nevertheless this does not completely solve our problem. For if the word "truth" is not used literally here, that is to say in the propositional sense, then why is this symbol used rather than any other? What is it which makes this particular word appropriate, and in some degree adequate? What causes us to use this particular metaphor?

According to all evidence, there is in the moment of mystic illumination an utterly irresistible sense or feeling of *conviction*. This, it is said, is the most powerful, compelling, coercive, overwhelming, experience of which the human mind is capable. It cannot be *denied* any more than the whirlwind, when it catches the traveler in its terrible breath, can be denied. The soul stands utterly convinced. Convinced of what? Of a proposition? Is it that the soul now believes something in the intellectual sense of the word belief, in the sense, that is, of accepting some predicate as attaching to some subject? If in this sense one asks what the soul is in that moment convinced of, the answer is, I believe, a total blank. There is nothing *of* which the soul is convinced except the conviction itself. Indeed the phrase "convinced *of* something" is applicable only to the conceptual intellect with its division of subject and object. The "something" is that which stands over against the mind as an object. And here there is nothing of that sort. Nevertheless there is the overwhelming sense of conviction. Now in the ordinary natural world, what one is convinced of is always a truth, or a proposition believed to be true; and what cannot be denied is also a truth. That the mystic should use the word truth to express his conviction is therefore entirely natural.

We turn to the consideration of God as the "Supreme Reality," the *ens realissimum* of the medieval theologians, the "ultimate reality" of some modern philosophers.

In all such phrases it is evident that the word "real" is being used in some symbolic way. For there is implied here a conception of degrees of reality. Some things, it is supposed, are more real than others, and God is the most real of them all. And this conception of degrees of reality is, of course, common among idealistic philosophers. There is, however, no literal sense of the word "real" in which there are degrees of the real. The word is a slippery one, and there are many senses in which it can be correctly used. All these common senses are literal in their signification, but none of them admits of the conception of degrees. We may give a few examples. Ghosts and unicorns, we say, are unreal. This means that they do not exist. "Reality," in this case, means the same as "existence." This is probably the primitive and original meaning of the word. But there are no degrees of existence. A thing either exists or it does not exist. It cannot half exist. Some other common senses of the word may be briefly mentioned. We say that the "real" shape of the penny is round, and that it only "appears" elliptical when held obliquely to the eye. Or we say that something is not "real" when it is an imitation—as a waxwork policeman at Madame

Tussaud's is not a real policeman. None of these derivative, though now literal, senses of the word has anything to do with the divine reality, and if we stick to the primitive meaning of the word as equivalent to existence, it cannot have a superlative such as "most real being" or "ultimate reality," because it has no degrees.

Light will be thrown on our problem if we consider why, in some religions and philosophies, the world—that is, the natural order—is called an illusion. Illusion is here the opposite of reality. God is real. The world is not real.

This idea is, of course, especially characteristic of Indian thought. In India we find the most extreme forms of it. The world is maya, illusion. Some Indian thinkers have gone so far as to say that the world "does not exist at all." But although this acosmism has not usually been characteristic of Christian theology, it would be a great mistake to suppose that it is purely Indian, or that the idea of the unreality of the world is not found among occidental thinkers whose backgrounds have been either Christian or pagan. In some shape or form, in some degree, it makes its appearance in the philosophies of Parmenides, Plato, Spinoza, Kant, Hegel, and the later British and American idealists. It is true that western thinkers do not usually proceed to the same extremes of the idea as do the Indians. No important western philosopher has said, so far as I know, that the world is "illusion," much less that it "does not exist at all." They use some milder term, such as appearance, or phenomenal existence, which does not import non-existence, but some comparatively low degree of reality. Plato thought that what he called "the world of sense" is half-real, if we may so paraphrase his statement that it partakes both of being and nonbeing, lying mid-way between the two.

Now the statement that the world is unreal (in any degree) has no meaning at all, if it is taken in any literal or factual way. It makes no sense. There is no common or literal meaning of the word "real" in which it is not merely nonsensical to say that the world is unreal. It would, for example, be empty verbiage to say that this paper on which I now write does not exist, since there is no test or criterion for the correct usage of the word "exist" the application of which would not give the result that this paper does exist. Thus "the world is unreal" cannot be a statement of fact at all. It is a mystical statement, and no mystical statement is a statement of fact. We have therefore to discover what the mystical sources of the doctrine are.

From the point of view of the natural order, the divine is an illusion. This is the doctrine of atheistic naturalism. The doctrine is not false. It is true. It is indeed the sole natural truth, the sole truth in so far as the realm of facts is concerned. From the point of view of the divine order, the natural world is an illusion. This is the doctrine of acosmism, which, within its own realm, is likewise the sole truth. And these two doctrines do not contradict one another, because they concern two different orders of being. Acosmism is to atheistic naturalism merely the reverse side of the coin.

As from within the eternal moment, there are two mystical sources of acosmism. First, the moment of mystic illumination contains all eternity and all infinity within itself. Outside of that one timeless moment of time, that swift passing vision of what never passes, there is and can be nothing, not even those other timeless moments which, in the life of the mystic himself, or in the lives of other mystics, have preceded or will follow it. Being the infinite, it has in itself all being, and there can be to it no other. This metaphysical conception of the infinite as that than which there is no other—which has nothing to do with the mere mathematical infinites, the endlessnesses, of time, space, and the number-series—is characteristic of mystical philosophies; and wherever it is found, as in the Upanishads, Spinoza, and Hegel, we know that these philosophies are rooted in mystical illumination, however rationalistic they may pretend to be, however unaware of their own mysticism their authors may be. If, then, there is nothing outside the eternal moment, there is and can be no world of space and time. The divine order is the sole reality, the natural order is non-existent.

This is the doctrine of pure acosmism, according to which the world does not exist at all. But although this extreme view has occasionally been expressed, it is not the ordinary mystic view. For it admits of no degrees of reality. There is for it only one reality, God; the rest is pure non-being. But mystical philosophies usually maintain, not that God is the only real, but that He is the *most* real, being; and not that the world is wholly non-existent, but that it is a half-reality—as in Plato—or that it has some indeterminate, but low, degree of reality denominated as "appearance," "phenomenal being," and the like. How does this diluted acosmism arise?

When the mystic descends from the eternal moment into the world of time, the things of space and time force themselves upon him again. He cannot wholly deny the fact of their "being there." But because the light and the memory of his supreme experience of the eternal floods over into his ordinary life, the things of space and time come to assume, for him, that ghost-like appearance which causes him to think of them as constituting a mere twilight world of shadows. The stronger his remembered sense of the eternal, the more illusory the world will seem to him. The more the vision fades, the more real will the world become. To common unmystical and unphilosophic men, too, a vague sense or feeling of the fluid emptiness, the impalpable unsolid mist-like character of the material world, comes in rare moments and in certain moods. And this can be explained only as an upsurge, from below the conscious level, of influences from the eternal moment buried in them.

Because the mystic lives in both worlds—speaks, as it were, from the standpoints of both—he is often involved in contradictions. From the standpoint of the eternal order it is true that there is no natural world. From the standpoint of the natural order, it is true that there is no divine world. So long as the two orders are kept separate, there can be no contradiction. But if the mystic allows the one to run, as it were, into the other in his consciousness, contradiction arises. The mystic—and we must remember that this means every one of us—must reconcile the contradiction as best he can. In order to do so, he conceives the idea of degrees of reality, and declares that the temporal world is a mere appearance, a half-reality, an illusion, a shadow-world, having that kind of semi-reality which shadows and dreams have—things which are, and yet are not.

Common men—those in whom the divine is more or less submerged—do not originate such views of the space-time world. But they show that there is within them the submerged potentiality of these views by the fact that, when they hear them, they receive them without incredulity. If they were sheer natural beings, if there were within them no divine—on our view, of course, there exists no such thing as a sheer natural being, because the divine intersects the natural at every point of the universe—they would perceive at once that such statements as "the world of sense is only half-real" are, from the point of view of the natural order, pure nonsense, senseless words. But anyone who has taught young and unsophisticated students Plato's *Republic,* or the Upanishads, knows that on the contrary they receive such views readily, sympathetically, and often with a kind of awe—because there is something in themselves which answers back.

There is a second, perhaps even more powerful, mystical source of acosmism and of the doctrine of degrees of reality. The eternal moment is experienced as the supreme value. It is that transcendent value which gives rise to the symbols blessedness, love, peace, righteousness. Now this supreme value of God is contrasted by the mystic with the worthlessness of this world. The worthlessness of the world is a common enough thought. Worldly pleasures have always been declared, both by mystics and by ordinary moralists, to be unworthy. They are glittering fantasies, baubles, deceitful, turning to ashes in the mouth. (Note the close connection between deceitfulness and illusion.) Everyone is familiar with such phrases. And if it be said that this condemnation of the world, whether by the mystic or by the potential mystic, is that very error which is the root of asceticism, and that the followers of an activist and dynamic religion will repudiate it, we need not deny this, except to say that repudiation, if it means total rejection, is too strong a word. The true religious doctrine is that the world is both to be denied and not to be denied. At the very least, you cannot actively rebuild the world until you have first rejected it as it is. And if we speak here of the worthlessness of the world, we are speaking no doubt of only a half of the truth, and taking it in separation from its complement. Let this be understood in what follows.

The world, then, is worthless trash. This is seen by all men, more dimly or more clearly, but with supreme and absolute clarity only by the mystic. It is essentially a religious insight, and cannot come to a man save through his religious consciousness. In so far as common men dimly perceive it, this perception is an influence of the divine moment in themselves. It cannot proceed from the natural consciousness. It is true that it has a naturalistic counterpart. It is a mere matter of experience that pleasures often deceive, in the sense that a man may seek happiness in a certain end, and find that it yields him more unhappiness than pleasure. Such ends are then declared worthless, and there may arise from this a general sense of the valuelessness of material things. And this natural insight may ape the religious insight, and be mistaken for it. But it proceeds from a contrast between a sought happiness and a found unhappiness, whereas the religious insight is founded on a contrast between the blessedness of the eternal moment and the unblessedness of the natural order. Happiness is a purely natural concept, whereas blessedness is an idea derived exclusively from the divine order. Happiness is no doubt the naturalistic counterpart of the divine blessedness. But because blessedness as such is wholly absent from the natural order—common men may in varying degrees experience it, but they do so as potentially divine beings, and not as natural beings—there can be in the natural order no contrast between the blessedness of the divine and the unblessedness of the world, and therefore no doctrine of the worthlessness of the world as this is understood by the mystic consciousness.

Now there exists in the human mind an ineradicable tendency to identify value with reality—that is, if value is here understood as the supreme value of divine blessedness. This may be expressed in the equation

$$\text{Value} = \text{Reality}$$

from which is derived the equation

$$\text{Unvalue} = \text{Unreality}$$

Evidences of this are easy to find in the world's literature. We may give a few examples. They are all found, it will be noted, in philosophies which have a mystical source, explicit or concealed. For Plato the most real existences are the "forms." They are the realities as against the unreality, or the half-reality, of the world of sense. But the forms are also the only truly valuable beings. Each is the "perfection" of the things which participate in it. The world of forms shines, in the philosophy of Plato, with a divine light. Here at once, then, reality and value are associated, equated. But this is not all. There is a hierarchy of forms. The forms stand, rank on rank, one above the other. And that form which stands at the apex of the pyramid, as the most real of all real beings, is the form of the Good, that is to say, the form of Value. Thus the most real and the most valuable are explicitly identified. It is also to be noted that there is in the philosophy of Plato absolutely no logical reason why he places the form of the Good at the top of his hierarchy. Mere logic would perhaps demand that the form of Being or of Existence, the common element of all things, should be placed at the top. Plato's procedure is a sheer irruption of the mystical consciousness into the middle of his logic.

Spinoza writes the equation of value with reality explicitly into his system. "By reality and perfection," he says "I understand the same thing." [2] It is true that he professes to use the word "perfection" only as a synonym for wholeness or completeness, and that, taken in this way, it is not a value term. For there are two senses of the word "perfect," one of which is its ethical sense, while the other is ethically neutral. The latter sense is found in such an expression as "a perfect circle." We do not mean that the circle is morally virtuous, but only that it is completely circular. There is here no value connotation at all. And if we should say "the devil is perfectly evil," no one would suppose that we meant to praise the devil for his goodness. It is professedly in this ethically neutral sense of wholeness or completeness that Spinoza uses the word "perfection" when he identifies it with reality. Yet it is easy to perceive that Spinoza, when he speaks of Substance or God as perfect, unconsciously, and doubtless against his own intention, imports into it a strong value meaning. For him, as for all philosophers whose thought is rooted in mysticism, God is blessedness, and blessedness is perfection, and perfection is reality. As is the case with Plato's form of the Good, we have here, in Spinoza's doctrine of perfection, an irruption of mysticism into the middle of a system professedly logical and—in Spinoza's case—rigidly rationalistic.

The modern absolute idealists afford another example of the identification of value with reality. The Absolute is, for them, the source of values, and even value itself.

From the equation, unvalue = unreality, there follows easily, of course, the doctrine of acosmism, the unreality of the world. From this point of view "the world is unreal" is a value judgment, the meaning of which is simply that the

[2] *Ethics*, part II, definition VI.

world is unblessed, or that it is worthless. We need hardly remind the reader that "the world is God's handiwork" is also a religious doctrine. It is the complement of the worthlessness of the world, which saves the latter from the error of asceticism.

It is worth noting that the unreality of the world is always especially connected with its character as a *flux*. In Plato's doctrine it is always on the becoming of the world that the predicate of unreality is fastened. Being is real, becoming, because it participates both in being and in non-being, is the half-real. In Indian thought, too, it is especially the fleetingness of things which makes them unreal. And the unreality of time has always been a favorite doctrine of idealistic philosophers. Although space and matter are for them logically just as unreal as time is, yet it is to the unreality of time that they always in the end seem to turn with a peculiar emphasis. These facts are not difficult to understand. For if the illusoriness of the world means in the end its worthlessness, even its evilness, it is the impermanence and transiency of things which seems to most men to rob them of value. For although time and change on the one side bring values to birth, so that the beauty of the flower, the song of the bird, the love of a man and a woman, come into being as parts of the chain of causes and effects which is the temporal order, yet on the other side time and change are seen as the destroyers of value. They take away from us all that we love. They bring sorrow. They bring to an end the beauty of the flower, the song of the bird, the love of man and woman. If they bring light, they also bring darkness. If they bring life, they also bring death. They are at once the creators and the destroyers. Logically speaking, it is absurd, even childish, to emphasize the one aspect more than the other. Men, however, are ruled by imagination and feeling rather than by logic. And for some reason, perhaps founded in that essential pessimism which is, after all, deeply rooted in man, the destructive aspect of time and change has always forced itself more vividly and poignantly on the human imagination than has their creative aspect. The passing away of things saddens us more than the bringing to birth of things gladdens us. The passage of time means to most men primarily the loss of dear ones, the onset of old age, death. Therefore the flux of the world is, in the imagination of men, deeply identified with the evil of the world, the inner worthlessness of things. Hence if unreality means worthlessness, it is above all time and change which are felt to be unreal.

We may, of course, inquire further regarding the mystic's identification of reality with value. No doubt it is a fact that he does identify the two. And this mere fact is all that we have so far shown. We quoted evidence to show that it is a fact. And we spoke of it as "an ineradicable tendency of the human mind." But if we leave it so, this ineradicable tendency will appear as a mere brute fact, a peculiar psychological twist of the human mind, even an irrational error. For there does not seem on the face of it to be any connection between the two terms "value" and "reality." A thing is not, as such, unreal because it is bad; nor real because it is good. Unfortunately, many evil things *are*, while many good things *are not*. What possible reason is there, then, for the mystic equation of value with reality?

No doubt a purely naturalistic explanation can be given. This will take the form of a psychological analysis. It will probably in the end find the explanation in wishful thinking. Men wish that evil were not. So they declare that it is not. It is unreal. And they wish that goodness were. So they declare that it is. It is the only true reality.

Naturalistic explanations are, as we have seen, true in their own kind. And therefore we shall not hesitate to accept whatever a well-founded psychology may tell us regarding the origin and cause of the mystic doctrine. But there is a deeper explanation of which the naturalist, as such, knows nothing, because it is rooted in the divine moment. Why is that which has the character òf blessedness the only reality, so that the unblessed—which is the natural order—is unreal? Because the blessed is also the infinite. But outside the infinite there is nothing. All else is illusion. Therefore outside the blessed there is nothing. That which is unblessed is illusion. Thus the axiological derivation of acosmism as a value judgment rests in the end on its metaphysical derivation, and appears only as a new aspect of this latter.

But now there descends upon this acosmic philosophy a strange and even ironical fate. Its assertion of the unreality of the world is not a statement of fact. It is a purely mystical doctrine. But it is stated in the form of a proposition. It has clothed itself in the conceptual language of the intellect, which is the language of fact. The disaster which comes upon it is that *it is mistaken for a statement of fact.* Not only the common man and the rationalistic philosopher make this mistake. There is reason to believe that even the mystic himself often, if not always, makes it. For he, as an inhabitant of the natural world, is no better, no cleverer, than another. He is liable to the same confusions, the same intellectual errors and semantic muddles, as other men. The mystic is indeed to be profoundly honored by us who are of baser clay. He belongs to a higher race, a race of supermen—though whether this means that the human race in general will at some future epoch evolve, reach upward, to his level, who can say? He is a divine being—at least in the supreme moments of his life—having walked with God. But though we must therefore profoundly reverence him, this does not mean that we are to accept blindly whatever he says, even in direct report of his experience, much less in his intellectual and philosophical theories based upon that experience. His experience is ineffable. And the ineffable is infallible—so long as it remains silent. But now he *speaks.* In doing so he frames logical propositions and concepts. He has handed himself over to the judgment of reason, rendered himself liable to

all the confusions, the tortuous mazes, the errors, the fallacies, to which the rational intellect is heir. There is no guar-
antee that he is an especially able, clever, or intellectual man.
Many who are his spiritual inferiors will far excel him in
intellectual power and logical acumen. It is therefore not
any matter for surprise if he, along with practically all other
men, should himself mistake his mystical doctrine that the
world is unreal for a statement of fact. He is the victim of
his own language. Has he not said "the world is unreal"?
Here is the subject, the predicate, and the copula. Is not
this statement just like "the tree is green," "the box is heavy,"
or any other factual statement, true or untrue? Must not
this also, then, the unreality of the world, be a fact?

This is but a particular case of the general principle that
all religious propositions are symbolic, but come to be taken
literally. For literal language and the language of fact are
identical. This is everywhere the trap which lies in the path
of the religious consciousness. It mistakes its own utterances
for literal statements of fact. Its doom is then sealed. For
always in the end it turns out that the alleged facts are not
facts, but fictions. And the discovery of this, whether by
science, or philosophy, or merely by common sense, is the
triumph of scepticism.

This is probably one of the causes of the ill-repute into
which idealistic philosophies, such as those of Hegel and
Bradley, dominant in England and America at the end of
the nineteenth century, have since fallen. Their assertion
that the world is appearance, not reality, was taken as a factual statement, not only by their opponents, but by the idealistic philosophers themselves. The battle was fought out on
the plane of this assumption. And, that being so, the issue
could not be in doubt. For to say in the literal sense that the
world, this paper, this chair, the sun, the moon, are unreal,
is palpable nonsense. The opponents of idealism made short
work of their enemies. Idealism is now—at any rate in Anglo-

Saxon lands—a despised and out-of-date creed—though it still has, of course, a few followers.

Although the mystic himself falls, like other men, into the trap, yet the philosopher is much more likely to do so than the pure mystic. For the religious consciousness of the latter works in the open daylight. The divine moment is in him self-realized, fully conscious. He knows, or should know, what it is. But the philosopher is as a rule an unconscious mystic. On the surface of his mind he is a rationalist. His mysticism, that is to say the eternal moment in him, is deeply submerged in the unconscious. Hence he may be quite unaware of the spring from which come his insights. Finding them in his consciousness, not knowing that they are upthrusts from a hidden source, he takes them to be due to the workings of his conceptual and logical intellect, and therefore takes the propositions in which they issue, such as that the world is unreal, to be logical, literal, and factual.

Reference was made above to the idealists of the nineteenth century. But this reference was not meant to imply that it was they who first fell into the literalist error. It has been, on the contrary, an almost universal phenomenon among philosophers in all ages. For example, Plato [3] and Spinoza, equally with the latter-day idealists, evidently took their belief in the unreality of the temporal order to be factual in character. So also the Indian philosophers generally took their acosmism to be factual.

This has had one extraordinary, even fantastic, result, namely the production, by a long line of philosophers stretching from Parmenides and Zeno to Bradley, of ingenious

---

[3] It is true that one often does not know, with Plato, what is meant as fact, and what as myth. But at least Plato, who was not too troubled about the distinction, always writes as if his doctrine of the semi-reality of the world were factual. That he supposed it is, or let it be thought that he supposed so, is evidenced by the circumstance that he used logical arguments to prove it. One uses arguments only to prove what one believes to be a fact.

logical arguments intended to *prove* that the world is unreal. For philosophers believed that its unreality is a fact. But if it is, it is certainly a very strange and surprising fact, violently at variance with the plain evidence of the senses and the reason, likely to be disputed and even ridiculed by those who hear it uttered. Therefore the philosopher, puzzled and perplexed, casts about him to find proofs that his doctrine is true, that it is, in other words, a fact. If he were aware that his doctrine, being mystical, is not a fact, he would not, of course, seek proofs for it. Where any set of statements is recognized as being of the nature of myth or symbolism, it would be absurd to try to prove them. Would any admirer of Bunyan try to show that his story of the pilgrim is historical? Thus the production by philosophers of proofs of the unreality of space, time, and the temporal world generally, is a direct result of their mistaking of their mystical propositions for factual propositions.

There could scarcely be a more ludicrous spectacle than that of Mr. F. H. Bradley and Mr. G. E. Moore *arguing* as to whether time is real or not, producing reasons and counter-reasons. And it is scarcely fair to blame Mr. Moore, when he argues that time is real, or that physical objects do actually exist, for his total lack of insight into the inner meaning and mystical significance of the idealistic doctrine, since Mr. Bradley, who argues that time is unreal, is equally in the dark as to the true meaning of his own doctrine. All one can say is that in Mr. Bradley there is at least the dim light of an intuition, though he does not know what it means, while in Mr. Moore there is apparently no intuition at all.

It follows from these considerations that all arguments which have ever been proposed—from the time of Zeno to the present day—to prove the unreality of the world, *must* be fallacious. They seek to show that the world is self-contradictory, and therefore cannot exist. But the world does exist, and therefore it cannot be self-contradictory; and the arguments to show that it is self-contradictory must contain logical mistakes. To say this is one thing; to discover and expose the logical mistakes in detail is quite another. For the arguments are extremely subtle, ingenious, and confusing. The fallacies are, therefore, extremely difficult to detect. But a good deal has been done, in recent years, by philosophers, logicians, and mathematicians, to expose at least some of them; and we must believe that all are capable of being cleared up by the ordinary methods of intellectual analysis.

Needless to say, no arguments of the philosophers, logicians, or mathematicians, can ever disprove the pure mystical doctrine of the illusory character of the world as it exists in the religious consciousness. That consciousness lies in a region which is for ever beyond all proof and disproof.

CHAPTER 8 THE DIVINE CIRCLE

THE PURE RELIGIOUS CONSCIOUSNESS LIES IN A REGION WHICH is forever beyond all proof or disproof.

This is a necessary consequence of the "utterly other" character of God from the world, and of the "utterly other" character of the world from God. The eternal order is not the natural order, and the natural order is not the eternal order. The two orders intersect, but in the intersection each remains what it is. Each is wholly self-contained. Therefore it is impossible to pass, by any logical inference, from one to the other. This at once precludes as impossible any talk either of the proof or disproof of religion.

When philosophers and theologians speak of "proofs of the existence of God," or "evidences of Christianity," what they have in mind is always a logical passage from the natural order, or some fact in the natural order, to the divine order. They may, for instance, argue in the following way. Here is the world. That is a natural fact. It must have had a cause. Other natural facts are then pointed out which are supposed to show adaptations of means to ends in nature. Bees pollinate flowers. Surely not by chance, nor following any purpose of their own. Or the heart has the function—which is interpreted as meaning the purpose—of pumping the blood. This teleological mechanism was not made by us, and the purpose evident in it is not our purpose. Therefore the cause of the world must have been an intelligent and designing mind. Doubtless I have much over-simplified the argument, and this version of it might not be accepted by the theologian as a statement of it which is to his liking. Certainly it is not a full statement. That, however, is not the point. The point is that, however the argument is stated, it necessarily starts from the natural order, or from selected facts in the natural order, and ends with a conclusion about the divine reality.

In other cases the natural fact from which the argument starts may be some very astonishing occurrence, which we do not yet know how to explain, and which we therefore call a miracle. This is evidence, it is believed, of a divine intervention.

In all cases we use some fact or facts of the natural order as premises for our argument, and then leap, by an apparently logical inference, clear out of the natural order into the divine order, which thus appears as the conclusion of the argument. The point is that the premise is in the natural world, the conclusion in the divine world.

But an examination of the nature of inference shows that this is an impossible procedure. For inference proceeds always along the thread of some relation. We start with one fact, which is observed. This bears some relation to another fact, which is not observed. We pass along this relation to the second fact. The first fact is our premise, the second fact our conclusion. The relation, in the case of the deductive inference, is that of logical entailment. In non-deductive inferences other relations are used, of which the most common is that of causality. Thus, although the sun is now shining, and the sky is cloudless, I see that the ground is wet, and the trees are dripping with water. I infer that an April shower has passed over, and that it rained a few minutes ago. My inference has passed along the thread of a causal relation from an effect as premise to a cause as conclusion. To pass in this way from facts which are before my eyes, along a relational link, to other facts which are not before my eyes— which are inferred, not seen—is the universal character of inference.

But the natural order is the totality of all things which stand to each other in the one systematic network of relationships which is the universe. Therefore no inference can ever carry me from anything in the natural order to anything outside it. If I start from a natural fact, my inferential process, however long, can end only in another natural fact. A "first cause," simply by virtue of being a cause, would be a fact in the natural order. It is not denied that it might conceivably be possible to argue back from the present state of the world to an intelligent cause of some of its present characteristics—although I do not believe that any such argument is in fact valid. The point is that an intelligent cause of the material world, reached by any such inference, would be only another natural being, a part of the natural order. The point is that such a first cause *would not be God*. It would be at the most a demi-urge. I shall return to this point later.

If God does not lie at the end of any telescope, neither does He lie at the end of any syllogism. I can never, starting from the natural order, prove the divine order. The proof of the divine order must lie, somehow, within itself. It must be its own witness. For it, like the natural order, is complete in itself, self-contained.

But if, for these reasons, God can never be proved by arguments which take natural facts for their premises, for the very same reason He can never be disproved by such arguments. For instance, He cannot be disproved by pointing to the evil and pain in the world.

But if, by arguments of the kind we are considering, the divine order can never be proved, nevertheless God is not without witness. Nor is His being any the less a certainty. But the argument for anything within the divine order must start from within the divine order. The divine order, however, is not far off. It is not beyond the stars. It is within us—as also within all other things. God exists in the eternal moment which is in every man, either self-consciously present and fully revealed, or buried, more or less deeply, in the unconscious. We express this in poetic language if we say that God is "in the heart." It is in the heart, then, that the witness of Him, the proof of Him, must lie, and not in any external circumstance of the natural order. So far as theology is concerned, we had better leave the bees and their pollination of flowers alone.

That the divine cannot be made the subject of proof is merely another aspect of the truth that the mystical illumination is incapable of conceptualization. For this means that God is inaccessible to the logical intellect. The attempt to prove His existence is an attempt to reach Him through concepts, and is therefore foredoomed to failure. The doctrine of the negative divine implies the same conclusion. For its meaning is that the door to an understanding of God is barred against the concept, and therefore against logical argument. And all this comes to the same as saying that God is known only by intuition, not by the logical intellect.

Every religious proposition, not only that which asserts the existence of God, is derived from religious intuition, and is incapable of any other proof. This is true not only of all the creeds of all the great religions. It is true of all religious statements made anywhere—of the propositions, for instance, contained in this book. Either they are based on intuitions, or they are baseless. Neither can they be, by the reader, submitted to the test of any logical proof or disproof. Their appeal is in the end solely to the reader's own religious intuition.

It is easy to be mistaken about this. The reader may, of course, argue. He may say, for instance, "such and such a proposition, which is asserted in this book, agrees, or does not agree, with the Catholic faith; and therefore it is true, or false." And the Catholic theologians themselves argued, and continue to argue. But the Catholic faith itself is ultimately based on nothing else but intuition. Thus in any theological argument the ultimate premise must be an intuition. From that point on the argument will proceed by logical steps to its conclusion. But the intuition itself is incapable of being proved by any argument. This is more conventionally expressed by saying that theology is based on revelation, and that all theological reasoning takes place within the framework of revealed truth. For revelation and intuition are two words for the same thing. In this book, as in other theological writings, there are, of course, trains of reasoning. But they remain always within the circle of ideas whose ultimate basis is intuitive. Their purpose is to show that one such idea is consistent with another, or that a suggested idea is inconsistent with some other proposition already intuitively accepted. They never argue from the outside, that is, from the natural order, to the divine order.

It may be discovered that one proposition of the theological system contradicts another. This will be due to one of two causes. Either the contradiction is ultimate and irremediable, as in the doctrine of the Trinity—a condition which will be discussed in the next chapter—or, in the case of merely subordinate propositions, it will show that there has been some mistake in the interpretation of the intuitions at the base of the system. But if the system is internally self-consistent, then as a whole it stands or falls solely on the basis of its intuitive appeal. If it is taken as a whole, as a completed circle of ideas, there is no way in which it can be supported or attacked from the outside. A system of religious beliefs is a symbolic account of the divine order. Outside of the divine order there is nothing except the natural order. Therefore to say that the circle of ideas, which are thus symbolically expository of the divine order, cannot be supported or attacked from the outside, is the same as saying that no proof or disproof of them which takes as its premises facts within the natural order is possible.

Those beliefs about God, about eternity, about the divine order, about the ultimate divine nature of the world, which constitute the body of what we call religious beliefs, and which we have attempted to elucidate in the preceding chapters, possess in this way the character of circularity. Each of them may logically imply the others, but none of them, nor all of them taken together, are implied by anything outside their own circle. They constitute the divine circle. No doubt in our treatment of the divine circle in this book we have failed in sundry ways to exhibit the mutual implication of religious truths. There will be found in it inconsistencies, incoherences, dark places, obscurities. This will be the fault of our treatment, not of the truths themselves. The point to be seized is that, whether we have succeeded or failed in our exposition, all religious reasoning must, if it is truly understood, be circular. And this means that nothing in the divine order is ever either implied or contradicted by anything in the natural order; and that religious truth in general can never be either proved or disproved.

We must bear in mind that we are speaking here not of religion itself but of religious beliefs, that is to say, of those propositions by means of which the intellect seeks to interpret symbolically to itself that inner and ultimate experience which is religion itself. We may imagine the religious experience as a sun, below which, and depending from which, hangs the circle of religious ideas or propositions. It is unsupported from below, from the earth, that is, from the natural order. And it is these propositions which, we say, cannot be derived by deduction or induction from anything within the natural order. They are to be derived only from the religious experience. To say of religion itself that it cannot be deductively or inductively derived would be meaningless. For religion is the experience, not the beliefs. And it has no meaning to speak of deducing or proving an experience. It is only propositions which are the subject matter of proof, demonstration, argument.

It may be thought that there is something essentially irrationalistic in the assertion that religious truths are wholly known by intuition, never by reason. This is a very natural criticism. But it can be shown to be a mistake. For exactly the same situation will be found to exist in regard to the aesthetic consciousness. The close resemblance between the aesthetic and the religious spheres has already been noted, and at

what has here been said about the aesthetic consciousness. For it would all be generally admitted. Why, then, should this charge be leveled against the conception that religious truths are in the end all known only by religious intuition, and are incapable of being proved by reason?

We must, however, expect an objection from another quarter. Intuitions, it will be said, are notoriously variable. If they are not subjected to any rule of reason, we shall have a hopeless chaos of conflicting opinions, with no way of deciding which is right. There is some truth in this; but there is also considerable exaggeration, as well as a fundamental misunderstanding of the role of reason in knowledge. The element of truth is easily seen. There actually are many conflicting opinions in religion. Not only are there differences of opinion within the fold of the Christian religion, but there are also conflicting religions. It does not follow from this, however, that religious intuitions conflict, although I do not mean to assert that they never can. I have argued in Chapter 2 that the different religions are the products of different geographical, cultural, and historical conditions interacting with the same basic religious intuitions. The differences, that is to say, may lie in the interpretations, not in the intuitions themselves. If so, it is the rational element which is at fault, not the intuitive element. For interpretation is the work of the logical intellect.

One must point out, in any case, that exactly the same situation exists in the aesthetic sphere. Here also there are differences of opinion, not only about the aesthetic value of particular works of art, but also, and even more so, about ultimate aesthetic principles and the very nature of beauty itself. Such disagreements about the nature of beauty correspond to disagreements in religion about the nature of the divine being. There may be different and conflicting aesthetic intuitions in different men, but different opinions about art and beauty do not prove it. The evidence already quoted in Chapter 2 seems to render it likely that the human aesthetic consciousness, that is to say, aesthetic intuition, is everywhere unitary, and that differences are produced mainly by different environmental conditions. In any case, aesthetic propositions *are* derived from intuitions. Yet the supposed variability of intuitions is not alleged to render either art, or art criticism, worthless. Why, then, should it be supposed to render religion, or religious opinions, worthless? Of course conflicting religious opinions cannot all be true. But neither can conflicting aesthetic, political, economic, or even scientific opinions. And that there exists conflict of opinions within a sphere of human knowledge, does not render that entire sphere of knowledge valueless.

Religious intuitions, like aesthetic intuitions, are also capable of being refined and educated. And when they are so, they may be brought nearer together, so that conflict is diminished. A savage has his religious intuitions, which are to be respected. They are not the same as those of a civilized man, or at least he does not interpret them in the same way. But they can be purified and civilized. Even if intuitions vary, this does not mean that any one is as good as any other, so that they all cancel out. Here again the situation is the same in the aesthetic sphere. The savage's artistic impulses may be different from those of educated men. But they can be purified and refined. And they then presumably become better and more valuable.

Furthermore, religious intuitions are capable of supporting one another. Though each is in itself intuitive, the system of beliefs which has its source in them is subject to the ordering control of reason, in exactly the same way as are the scientific beliefs which are based on sense experience. The comparison between mystical experience and sense experience is a dangerous one for the reasons given in Chapter 3. But there is an analogy in the fact that science is an interpretation of sense experience, in the same way as religious beliefs are interpretations of mystical experience. Neither the sense experience nor the religious experience is in itself rational. The function of reason in both cases is the interpretation and the logical ordering of the interpretations. Logic never originates anything either in religion or science. It only orders beliefs which have originated from non-rational experiences, whether they be sensuous or religious or aesthetic. The objectivity of science is due to the fact that sense experiences are basically the same in all men, although some differences exist, not to the fact that the basic experiences upon which science builds its constructions, namely the sense experiences, are rational. In principle, exactly the same can be said of religion, although it is not maintained that the similarity of religious experience in all men is either as great, or as clearly verifiable, as are the similarities of their sense experiences.

It is noticeable that, in the climate of opinion of the present day, theologians and religious men generally place little reliance, if any, on the traditional proofs of the existence of God. In the Roman Catholic church they are still treated as important, but not, as a rule, in other communions—or at least not in the same degree. A common attitude among practical churchmen seems to be that while no emphasis should be placed on them, and while perhaps no one really knows whether they have any logical validity, they had better not be denounced or openly discarded, because it is impossible to know that they may not, at some time, or to some people, be of help. Their general neglect is not evidence of a decay of faith; rather the contrary. For it goes along with a growing realization that the witness of God is within the soul. Nevertheless it has not been uncommon for religious men to reject them altogether. David Hume, who subjected them to a merciless analysis, was, of course, a sceptic. But among religious men Pascal and Kant stand out as critics of them.

The opinion that a proof of the existence of God is a logical impossibility—which is here maintained—though it was held by Kant, cannot be attributed to Pascal. But he deplored the so-called proofs on the ground that they are so weak that they are calculated to produce atheism rather than faith. If they are used in the hope of convincing an unbeliever, the only result will be "to give grounds for believing that the proofs of our religion are very feeble." His famous saying that "the heart hath its reasons, which the reason knows not of," though it is objectionable in some respects, goes to the root of the matter. The heart, as distinguished from the head, is commonly the symbol for emotion as distinguished from abstract thought. Hence Pascal's sentence may suggest that religious experience is mere emotion, or even wishful thinking. There is, and should be, an element of emotion in religion, but it should not be emotionalism; and in any case the mystical experience is not rightly conceived as an emotion. For the word emotion usually connotes a purely subjective state of mind. But the deeper meaning of Pascal's saying is that religious belief is based upon direct intuitive experience, and not upon any logical proof.

Kant's "refutations" of the traditional proofs of the existence of God are, of course, famous. It is especially to be noted that he put them forward in the interests of religion, not in the interests of scepticism. He believed firmly in "God, freedom, and immortality." And even if his religion appears to us as dry, abstract, and formal, with little element of religious "feeling," it is nevertheless the fact that one of the main motives of his entire philosophy was to "save" religion from the sceptic. To many it may seem a questionable procedure to try to support religion by annihilating the proofs of it, by showing that they are nothing but a set of fallacies. The timid man clings to the proofs, thereby showing—we must be allowed to remark—his lack of faith. But there is no doubt that Kant's bold procedure was the right one. I do not mean that his refutations were conclusive. They are very obscure, and I suspect that they contain logical mistakes; in other words that they are not refutations at all. But his intention was right, and rested on the true

insight that the realm of the spirit lies beyond all possibility
of proof or disproof; that the divine order is wholly other
than the natural order, so that there is no logical passage from
the one to the other. He was right in perceiving that all
attempts to compromise between religion and scientific naturalism must in the end spell disaster for religion; that one
hundred per cent of what it claims must be granted to science,
and to religion one hundred per cent of what it claims; and
that this is possible only if the two orders, the natural and
the religious, are seen to be independent realms, each wholly
self-contained. The common attempts at reconciliation, well
worked in Kant's day and still fashionable in ours, in effect
place God and the world in the same order—as is done, for
example, if we conceive God as a "first cause," whereby
He is made merely the first member of that causal chain
which is the natural order—and then proceed to a division
of territory, whereby some part of this order is assigned to
religion and the other part to science, whether the division
be fifty-fifty or some other. It is to be feared that in our
own day some scientists suppose that religious beliefs, freedom, and perhaps even God, are made possible by the new
principle of the indeterminancy of the electron, that is to
say, by a discovery within the natural order.

The error of Kant's philosophy lay in its disregard of
mystical experience. For him, as for us, God is "utterly
other." In our philosophy this appears as the principle that
the eternal order and the temporal order, though they intersect, are wholly different, each self-contained. In Kant's
philosophy it appears as the complete separation of the phenomenal world and the noumenal world. God is relegated
to the noumenal world, which is Kant's equivalent of the
eternal order. But any such philosophy, if it conceives the
logical intellect as the sole organ of knowledge, necessarily
makes God unknowable. For the logical intellect operates
only within the natural order. Therefore the divine order
is unknowable to the logical intellect. This is perfectly

correct—it is the principle of the negative divine—and it is the conclusion which Kant reaches. But to make God completely unknowable is to make an end of religion—the opposite of Kant's intention. There must therefore be some way of knowing God other than by the logical intellect. This is religious intuition, which Kant fails to include in his system. It amounts to the same thing to say that the noumenal world is wholly unempirical, unless it can be experienced in intuition. And the failure to recognize intuition in his philosophy resulted in Kant's noumenal world being dismissed as unempirical by later philosophers.

The great error of the traditional proofs of the existence of God is that they take a symbolic truth for a literal truth, a truth of fact, and then try to prove that it is a fact. The religious doctrine speaks of God as a mind or person, purposively controlling the world for good ends, and filled with love for men and all creatures. This symbolic language is taken as stating literal facts, and then "evidences" of these facts are sought. The results are invariably disastrous for religion. The evidences are torn to shreds by the sceptic without difficulty, and it then seems to all the world as if religion has been destroyed, although, if religion were truly understood, it would be seen that it emerges entirely unscathed from these sceptical attacks.

For instance, it is desired to prove that God is good and loves His creatures. The only possible "evidences" for this, to be found in the natural order, will consist in the various "blessings" which men undoubtedly enjoy—in other words, the various good things which the world contains and the happiness which men often experience. But if these are pointed out, all the sceptic has to do is to point to the evil and misery in the world, most of which cannot by any conceivable stretch of imagination be attributed to man's own fault, although some can. (Presumably none of the agony suffered by animals can be thought of as due to their fault.) This is evidence on the other side, and entirely destroys the religious argument. For the conclusion which that argument seeks to reach is not that God is partly good, and partly evil, which is what would follow from an impartial balancing of the good and evil things in the world, but that God is wholly good. The only refuge of the religious man will consist in saying that, while the good in the world is evidence for God's goodness, the evil in the world is not evidence of His badness, but only of the fact that the existence of evil is for man a mystery and an insoluble problem. But obviously, from the point of view of logical argument, to which the religious man has foolishly committed himself, he cannot be allowed thus to quote the evidence which is in his favor, while refusing to take any account of the evidence against him, under the pretext that it is a mystery.

These defeats come upon religious men because they take their doctrines to be literal statements of fact, and therefore amenable to proof by argument. It must now be added that these attempts at proof not only fail of their purpose, and so do no good to religion, but that they positively degrade it. For their effect is to drag down the divine and the eternal from their own sphere into the sphere of the natural and temporal. As has already been pointed out many times, if we argue back along the chain of causes to a first cause, and call this first cause God, we thereby make Him merely one among other things in the world, that is, in the natural order. All the other alleged proofs have the same effect. They thus make God finite. For the natural order is the order of finite things. If God is related to other things as their cause, then He is finite, since the otherness of these other things limits His being. This is the result of taking God's causality in a literal sense—in the sense, that is, in which we say that heat is the cause of the boiling of water. This also places God in time, because the causal relation is a time relation. But if the causality of God is taken symbolically, then it plainly cannot be proved by going backwards along the causal chain, since this procedure implies the literal understanding of the causal concept.

It is a logical impossibility to pass by inference from the natural order to the divine order. But it is not, of course, a logical impossibility to pass from one thing in the natural order to another. Therefore it is not a logical impossibility that there should be evidences of a vast mind running the affairs of nature. All sorts of purely naturalistic suggestions of this kind are possible. We cannot be sure that the human mind is the largest in the universe. Nor are disembodied minds a logical impossibility. The earth might therefore be presided over by a great invisible mind, who might take orders from a still greater mind in charge of the solar system. This spirit might in turn be subordinate to another spirit which supervises the galaxy. The solar system might be a single atom—the earth a single electron spinning round the nucleus—in the blood stream of some vast animal, whose body is the entire material universe. Such fantasies could conceivably be true. But they are superstitions nonetheless, because they are groundless, gratuitous, and lacking in any foundation of evidence. The point, however, is that no such vast mind running the universe, or a part of the universe, however enormous, magnificent, powerful, intelligent, good, it might be, could be God. For it would be merely another natural being, a part of the natural order, or perhaps the whole of it. God so thought of is a superstition, a gigantic and perhaps benevolent ghost, an immense, disembodied, and super-earthly clergyman. And some such superstition is what is implied by all the supposed proofs of His existence.

We return to our position that there is no logical reasoning which will carry us from the natural order to the divine order. There is no such thing as natural theology. God is either known by revelation—that is to say, by intuition—or not at all. And revelation is not something which took place in the past. It takes place in every moment of time, and in every heart—although it reaches a climactic moment in the illumination of the great mystic.

This is also the solution of the old problem of the relation between faith and reason. God is known by faith, not by reason. But faith does not mean blindly believing propositions for which there is no evidence, or which are contrary to the evidence. It is degraded, when so conceived, into superstition or mere pig-headedness. Faith and intuition are one and the same thing. To discover God is the function of faith. But, reason, too has its function in the religious sphere. It has to interpret to the intellect the discoveries of faith in the only possible way, by means of symbolic propositions; and also to ensure that these symbolic propositions are mutually consistent and fall into an ordered system. This is the truth of the medieval view that reason operates within the framework set by faith and revelation. That reason must stay within the bounds set by revelation, must not contradict it, or seek to go behind it, means that the source of all divine truth is intuition, that reason has nothing to do with its origination, and can do no more than interpret the truths which intuition gives. This insight, correct in itself, is, of course perverted when it is made to mean that what some book or organization has said is to be blindly accepted "on faith," without examination.

CHAPTER 9 MYSTICISM AND LOGIC

ALTHOUGH THE THEOLOGICAL INTELLECT, IN ACCORDANCE with the conception of the divine circle, endeavors always to arrange its propositions in a self-consistent system, yet, in regard to the most fundamental and ultimate religious insights, this cannot be done. The first principle of logical reasoning is the law of contradiction, namely, that two propositions which contradict each other cannot both be true. Theology can follow this principle in its peripheral and subordinate assertions, those which are mere implications of its central core of insights. But this central core itself does not yield to this logical treatment. When we seek to logicize it, we find in it irreducible self-contradictions.

We may be inclined to express this by saying—as has often been said—that at the heart of things, in the very nature of the Ultimate itself, there is contradiction. We may make use of this mode of expression without objection. But it is not strictly accurate. For the Ultimate itself cannot be either self-contradictory or self-consistent. It is an indivisible one, without parts; whereas self-contradiction means the logical opposition of one part to another, while self-consistency means the logical harmony of one part with another. The Ultimate can be neither self-consistent nor self-contradictory, for both of these are logical categories. It is neither logical nor illogical, but alogical. What we should say, rather, is that the contradictions are in us, not in the Ultimate. They arise from the attempt to comprehend the Ultimate by logical concepts. The Ultimate rejects these concepts, and when we seek to force them upon it, the only result is that *our thinking* becomes contradictory.

But however we choose to express it, this is the same thing as the doctrine of the mystery of God. There are only two ways of understanding the concept of that mystery. One is to suppose that it means only that there are some truths about

God which the intellect has not yet found out, and perhaps never will find out, but which, so far as the essential nature of the intellect is concerned, could theoretically be discovered. The mystery of the Trinity might be solved by some kind of mathematics which is at present entirely beyond the world's greatest mathematicians. If certain conditions were present, if we lived long enough, if all possible information about the universe were at our disposal, if the human mind should, in the future, develop sufficient intellectual power and logical acumen, then God in His full nature might be known and comprehended; and all the apparent contradictions, which now develop when we try to understand Him, would be seen to disappear. God in that case is only accidentally a mystery, and His mystery is theoretically removeable. The other alternative, which is the one here asserted, is that the logical intellect is inherently and for ever incapable, owing to its essential structure, of understanding the Ultimate. This is the same as saying that the final secret of the world refuses to yield itself up to a mind whose principle is the logical law of contradiction, so that when such a mind attempts to understand it, contradictions result. According to this view, the mystery of God is essential, absolute, and irremovable.

Again, the mystery of God is the same as His incomprehensibility, affirmed in the Athanasian creed. According to the first interpretation, this affirmation of the creed is only an exaggeration, made presumably for the purpose of glorifying God—although it seems doubtful whether God is rightly glorified by the use of exaggerated language. According to the second interpretation, God's incomprehensibility is no exaggeration, but the very truth. It is inherent in the divine nature, absolute and essential to that nature, and therefore incapable of being modified or removed.

Again, this conception of the divine nature as incapable of being apprehended by the logical intellect is identical with the conception of God as the "utterly other," as wholly outside the natural order. In this formulation of the matter, also, either of the two interpretations may be used. According to the first interpretation, this utterly other nature of God is only another exaggeration. In that case, we should think of God as one among other things in the universe, although no doubt a vastly greater, nobler, more powerful being than any other. According to the second interpretation, to say that God is utterly other means that He is not a part of the universe, one thing among others, but that His being lies in a plane, order, or dimension, wholly different from the system of things which constitutes the natural order. This is exactly the same thing as asserting that God is not capable of being apprehended by concepts. For the concept is, in its very nature, that power of the mind by which it traces relations between one thing and another in the universe. And if God is not one among these things, then the logical intellect can never find Him.

There is still another antithesis with which our view, and the opposing view, can be identified. For our view, that God is utterly other, is also identical with the interpretation of religious truth as symbolic; and the opposite view is identical with the interpretation of it as literal. For if we take any religious proposition, such as "God is love," the literal interpretation of it will imply that there is a comparison between God's love and that of men. God's love is then greater only in degree, not in kind. And God Himself is only one loving personality among others. If, on the other hand, we take the proposition to be symbolic, then this will imply that there is no comparison at all between God's love and ours, that His love, and He himself, belong to a wholly different order from that in which we, in our natural moments in the time-order, live and move.

Thus our view may be stated in several different ways. We may express it by saying either that God is utterly other; or that the logical intellect is incapable of apprehending Him; or that the nature of the Ultimate is for us self-contradictory; or that God's mystery and incomprehensibility are absolute and inherent in His being; or that all religious propositions are symbolic. These diverse statements all imply each other, and in the end are merely different ways of saying the same thing. Consequently, the view contrary to ours may also be stated in a number of corresponding diverse ways, which, however, are really equivalent. It will assert that God, however much greater and nobler than other beings He may be, is different from them only in degree and not in kind, or, in other words, that He is not utterly other—unless this phrase be taken as a mere honorific; that a sufficiently evolved conceptual intellect could completely understand God, could resolve the contradictions which at present center round the attempt to do so; that His mystery and incomprehensibility are only relative; and that religious propositions are to be understood literally.

There is no doubt that the issue thus set out in different forms is the basic issue of this book; and that the more profound and instructed criticisms of our conceptions will center round it. On this issue we stand or fall. I have attempted throughout the preceding chapters, but especially in Chapter 5, to give the answers to the criticisms which arise from the adoption of the opposite point of view. In this final chapter I shall endeavor to support our view by means of certain indirect considerations.

The question cannot be decided by argument, nor is the view which we have affirmed capable of being "proved," if by proof we mean a logical passage from things in the natural order to things in the divine order. Religious truths depend wholly on religious intuitions. In other words, our appeal must be only to basic human intuitions, not to any "facts." And my contention is that the interpretation of religion which has here been set out accords with, and that the opposite interpretation jars upon, and is discordant and disharmonious with, the following specific intuitions, to wit:

(1) The intuition which expresses itself in the proposition that God is a mystery beyond all human understanding.

(2) The connected intuition which expresses itself in the proposition that the blessedness of God is "the peace of God *which passeth all understanding.*"

(3) The intuition which expresses itself in the proposition that there is no blessedness in finite things, but only in the infinite—which is false if blessedness is taken to mean anything comparable with natural happiness.

(4) The intuition which expresses itself in the proposition that God is infinite; which He cannot be, if He is one among other things, a being standing in relation with the things of this world.

(5) The intuition which expresses itself in the proposition that God is eternal; which He cannot be unless He belongs to an order wholly other than the order of time.

(6) The intuition which expresses itself in the proposition that God is the Void; which cannot mean anything except that His being is a total blank to the logical intellect, and that He cannot be found by proceeding along the threads of the web of inter-relationships among the existences which constitute the natural order.

I pass now to another set of considerations which support the same conclusions. I shall show first that the assertion that there is contradiction in the Ultimate itself, or rather— more correctly put—that the attempt to state the nature of the Ultimate in logical propositions necessarily produces contradictions, is itself based upon an intuition; and, secondly that, in consequence, contradictions necessarily break out in all philosophies whose source and inspiration is mysticism, and that all attempts to resolve these contradictions necessarily fail.

We must distinguish between what we will call pure religious mystics,—such men as Eckhart, Tauler, St. John of the Cross, the authors of the Upanishads,—and philosophers, such as Spinoza, Hegel, Bradley. Strictly speaking, of course, there is no such thing as a "pure" mystic, since all mystics are also rational beings, and therefore tend to philosophize. But there is a rough distinction between the two sorts of men, which will be readily understood. The first assertion of the last paragraph—that contradiction in the Ultimate is itself a religious intuition—refers to those whom we have called pure mystics. The second assertion—that philosophies based on mysticism always contain irresoluble contradictions—refers to those who are more commonly classed as philosophers.

As to the first point, the reader of mystic utterances can scarcely fail to be struck by the fact that the mystic consciousness constantly chooses to express itself in paradoxical language. Two or three examples of this will suffice to illustrate the point, although a large catalogue of them could easily be collected.

According to Jacob Boehme, the Eternal Yes and the Eternal No lie together in the ultimate nature of God. Conflict, division, contradiction are in the nature of things, and are necessary to existence. No doubt the words Yes and No are used in a poetical way, and are not meant as logical concepts. But why does Boehme, if he wishes to speak poetically of God, select from all the words in the dictionary these two particular words? Plainly because they serve to bring to a sharp point, a vivid focus, the idea of the contradictoriness of the Ultimate.

The words of Eckhart, already quoted in another connection, "Thou shalt love God as He is, a non-God," are self-contradictory. All ways of expressing the negative divine, such as that God is "the nameless Nothing" involve contradiction.

The doctrine of the Trinity is, of course, another example.

Having given these examples from Christian sources, we may now quote two from the Upanishads. These writings, which are perhaps the earliest mystical utterances in history, are full of self-contradictory language. Thus we read:

> "That One, though motionless, is swifter than the mind.
> Though immoveable, It travels faster than those
>   who run.
> It moves, and It moves not." [1]

These words, again, are poetical. Obviously they are not meant to refer to physical motion. What, then, do they mean? Motion, of course, symbolizes the creativeness of God, which is an element of the positive divine, while the absence of motion symbolizes His unchangeableness, which is an element of the negative divine. But why are the two contradicting predicates thus thrust together in a single sentence of six words, "It moves and it moves not"? We all of us contradict ourselves at times. But we do so by mistake. Our contradictory statements lie, as a rule, far apart. I say one thing, perhaps, on page fifty of my book, and the opposite on page one hundred. As soon as this is pointed out, I admit that I have made some mistake. But the contradiction in the Upanishad is obviously deliberate, and one can even sense that there is a certain glorying in it, as if it were part of the essential message of its author. And this is in fact the case. It cannot be doubted that it means to affirm self-contradiction of the Ultimate.

After this we are not surprised to find another Upanishad asserting of Brahman that it "is both being and non-being." [2] Here the words chosen are not poetical. They constitute a direct and literal repudiation of the logical law of contradiction, so far as the application of that law to God is concerned.

We noticed that Whitehead's words, quoted on the first page of this book, exhibit, when speaking of the ultimate "something," a tendency to paradox and self-contradiction.

[1] Isa Upanishad.
[2] Mundaka Upanishad.

Whitehead is not what would ordinarily be called a mystic. But he is an exceptionally intuitive writer. His severest critics admit that his writings—however they may criticize them on various scores—are full of sudden flashes of insight. I remarked in the first chapter that the particular words there quoted plainly well up from his own religious experience. It is probably not the case that he explicitly intended, as did the writer of the Upanishad, to affirm that the Ultimate is self-contradictory. But this very fact makes the evidence of his words the more impressive. It shows that this ultimately contradictory character, which lies in the heart of things, forces itself upon his intuitive utterance whether he intends it or not, perhaps even in spite of his intentions.

Except in the case of Whitehead, we have been speaking so far of those whom we called pure religious mystics. If we now turn to some of those who would ordinarily be called philosophers, rather than mystics, we find that in certain cases the source of their inspiration—whether they know it or not—is mystical; and that wherever this is the case, contradictions always break out in their philosophies, in spite of their efforts to suppress or conceal them. The contradictions *cannot* be got rid of, because they lie at the very center of the mystical source from which these philosophies proceed. But the philosopher is usually not aware of this situation. He therefore struggles to rid himself of the contradictions. For to have contradictions in his system is contrary to his professional code. His struggles are always futile, but for us very instructive.

The professional philosopher is, as such, a rationalist. His chosen organ of knowledge is reason. His attempt is always to give a rational, logical explanation of the world. He is therefore committed to the view that the world is, even in its ultimate essence, rational and self-consistent. If he remains wholly true to this point of view, if he is through and through rationalistic, if, that is to say, he suppresses—so far as his official philosophy is concerned—the eternal moment within himself; or if it is so far buried in the darkness of his sub-conscious that it exerts no noticeable influence in the upper layers of his mind, then, in these cases, he will become a naturalist. For naturalism which, when it is fully developed, is atheistic naturalism, is the only purely rational philosophy. For reason—which is another name for the conceptual intellect—is, as such, aware only of the natural order. It is the part of the mind which traces relations between things; and this fact confines it to the natural order, since the natural order includes all relations and related things and nothing else. But if, instead of remaining a pure rationalist, the philosopher admits into his mind, and into his philosophic scheme, an influx of religious intuition, a curious result ensues. The rationalism will lie on the surface of his mind, immediately to hand, obvious to himself. The mystical influx comes from below, and influences his mind secretly. Either he is not aware of it at all, or he is aware of it only as vague feeling, a persistent bent of his thought to take certain directions. As a result of this mystic inflow, contradictions are perpetually breaking out in his philosophy. Being a professional rationalist, who cannot admit contradictions, he fights to overcome them by purely logical means. The lesson to be learned from him is that he never can do this, and that, if the contradictions are suppressed in one place, they always burst out again in some other place.

I will give four examples of this, the Vedanta, Spinoza, Hegel, and Bradley.

All these philosophies assert, each in its own way, the proposition that the Ultimate is one and infinite. Because this is a mystical doctrine, it necessarily gives rise to a contradiction in any philosophical attempt at a rational understanding of it. The precise contradiction, to which it leads, is that the world both *is* and *is not* identical with God, Brahman, Substance, the Absolute—or whatever the Ultimate is called. This contradiction is ultimate and irresoluble.

It arises because of the following logical necessity. The

Ultimate, being infinite, can have nothing outside it. Therefore the world cannot fall outside it. There cannot be any
difference, any otherness, as between the Absolute and the
world. Therefore the world *is* the Absolute. But the Ultimate, being one, is relationless, without parts, without division, without manyness. The world, on the other hand, is the
arena of manyness, division and relation. Therefore it *is not*
the Absolute, is not contained in it, falls outside it.

We have to show that this contradiction makes its appearance in the Vedanta, Spinoza, Hegel, and Bradley, and that
it never is, and cannot be, resolved.

The Vedanta may, of course, be taken either as pure
mysticism or as philosophy, but this point is unimportant.

In the Vedanta, the world both *is* and *is not* God. There
is identity in difference. The identity is usually asserted in
the Upanishads by the device of giving a catalogue of natural
objects and asserting that all of them are Brahman. For
instance,

> "Thou are the fire,
> Thou art the sun,
> Thou art the air,
> Thou art the moon,
> Thou art the starry firmament,
> Thou art Brahman Supreme:
> Thou art the waters—thou,
> The Creator of all!
>
> Thou art the dark butterfly,
> Thou art the green parrot with red eyes,
> Thou are the thunder cloud, the seasons, the seas."

But the otherness of the sun and the moon, their non-
identity with Brahman, is implied in the doctrine of maya.
The sun and the moon cannot be, as such, simply as they
are in their natural characters, Brahman. For as such they
are illusion, not reality, and Brahman is pure reality. And

though Sankara, and other later philosophers, struggle to overcome the contradiction by logical means, it is impossible for them to do so.

The doctrine of identity in difference is also plainly required by the assertion of the identity of atman, the individual self, with Brahman, the universal self. They are at the same time one and different.

It is outside the scope of this book to enter upon technical details of the philosophies of Spinoza, Bradley, and Hegel. But the following points may be made briefly.

Spinoza is a professional rationalist, but any sensitive reader can detect an influx of mystical thought and feeling in his philosophy. And his concepts of the infinity of God, blessedness, the intuitive apprehension of God, and the unreality of time, all indicate this. According to Spinoza the universe is a single infinite Substance having an infinite number of attributes, of which two, extension and thought, are known to us. Particular finite things are "modes" of one or other of the attributes. Spinoza specifically identifies Substance with God, the ultimate reality. What we have called "the world" is represented in his philosophy by the attributes and modes. Spinoza says that the attributes "constitute" Substance—that is to say, God *is* the world. On the other hand, it is evident that Substance is something more than the attributes and modes; it is a substratum lying beyond or below them. That is to say, God is different from the world.

Bradley, of course, is a post-Hegelian, but it will be convenient to mention him before Hegel. According to Bradley, the world of space and time is full of contradictions, and is therefore not reality, but appearance. The Absolute is beyond space and time. It is infinite, in the usual mystical sense of being that than which there is no other. The world, therefore, is not other than the Absolute, but identical with it. Yet it is also obviously different. Space and time, for instance, are not in the Absolute, since they are self-contradictory, and the Absolute must be—according to Bradley—self-consistent. Yet space and time must be, in some way, in the Absolute, since there is nothing outside it. Thus space and time are both in the Absolute and not in it. How can this be? Bradley says that they do not appear in the Absolute "as such," that is to say, in their natural characters as they are for us, but absorbed, transformed, transfigured in such a way that their contradictions disappear. How this can be, we do not know. It is "somehow, we know not how." This latter phrase, which occurs on page after page of Bradley's book, must be taken by us as representing the despair of reason in its attempt to comprehend the Ultimate by means of its logical concepts. This is the lesson we are to draw from Bradley.

We see thus that philosophies which start from the mystical intuition of God as infinite necessarily lead into the contradiction that God both is and is not the world. Hegel, no more than Spinoza, will admit that his philosophy is mystical. On the surface, he is an ultra-rationalist. He supposes that he can logically deduce all the main characters of the world from the nature of the Absolute. That reality and rationality are the same thing is his slogan. But he perceives clearly that the rationality of the Ultimate cannot be shown by means of the traditional logic, whose essential principle is the law of contradiction. He perceives clearly the contradiction of the Ultimate, as both identical with, and different from, the world, which is implicit in his predecessors. He proposes a desperate remedy, the invention of a wholly new kind of logic, whose essential principle is to be "the identity of opposites." This new logic will solve the contradictions.

According to this logic, being is identical with non-being, although they are at the same time entirely different and contradictory. The same is true of many other familiar pairs of opposites, such as the many and the one, the finite and the infinite. It is true, indeed, of all opposites. Hegel not merely asserts this. He tries, with extraordinary ingenuity, to prove it in detail of each pair of opposites as it comes up. The point is that he tries to show it *logically*. He does not put it forward as a mystical intuition. Thus he attempts to show, by logic alone, exactly how and why being implies non-being, is in fact identical with non-being, although they are different.

This, obviously, is exactly what mysticism and mystical philosophies, such as the Vedanta, Spinoza, and Bradley, require, if it is to be shown that their truths are intelligible to reason, and not only to intuition. Hence Hegel must be credited with attempting to found a logic of mysticism— although he might himself have repudiated this description, owing to his belief that he was a pure rationalist. Had he succeeded, he would have healed the ancient schism between mysticism and logic. The purely logical intellect rejects, and must reject, mysticism, because of its contradictions. It may admit that the mystic illumination is a noble emotion. But it is compelled to reject the claim of the mystic to a vision of reality. The mystic, on the other side, tends to reject logic, claiming that his vision is "above reason." Yet both mysticism and logic have paramount claims on the human mind. Their warfare appears, therefore, as a civil strife within human mentality. Hegel's success, if he had achieved it, would have meant the end of this strife. But it would also have meant the end of the mystery of God, which we hold, on the contrary, to be of the essence of religion.

It is not possible in this book to discuss the technical reasons why Hegel's effort must be held to have been a logical failure. We must content ourselves with the remark that his own followers have, since almost immediately after his death, admitted its failure. None of them has attempted to use his logical method. Their endeavor has been to preserve the idealistic doctrine of the master without its peculiar logic. This, for example, is what Bradley tried to do. We have already seen what the consequence for Bradley was. The contradiction of the identity of opposites, which Hegel tried to solve, lies open and naked in Bradley's philosophy, an unhealed sore. Thus the conclusion follows: if you allow entrance of the mystic illumination into your philosophy, then either you must accept a logic of the identity of opposites (Hegel's or some other like it), or you must admit that the Ultimate is incapable of being comprehended by the conceptual intellect. And this is the same as admitting that absolute otherness of God for which we have contended. The lesson of the futile struggles of philosophers to solve their contradictions, and of the final failure of the Hegelian logic, is that for which mystics have always contended, that the Ultimate cannot be comprehended by reason. And this is the same as saying that God is utterly other, that the mystery and incomprehensibility of God are absolute and irremovable, that all religious language is symbolic and not literal. And these are the main contentions of this book.

INDEX

Absolute, The, 25, 26, 84, 85, 161, 162, 163, 164
Absolute Idealism, 128, 132-133
Abyss, 9, 30
Acosmism, 77, 78, 123, 124, 125, 128, 131, 133
Adequacy of religious symbols, 92 ff.
Aeschylus, 16, 17
Aesthetic consciousness, 117, 141, 145
Albertus Magnus, 11
Alexander, Samuel, 81
Aquinas, Thomas, vi
Art, 6, 18, 117, 142-144
Asceticism, 108, 129
Athanasius, creed of, 37, 42, 154
Atheism, vi, 9, 54, 78, 147
Atman, 23, 163
Augustine, 11

Being, 8, 10, 24, 26, 50, 51, 59, 67, 164
Bentham, 106
Berkeley, 57
Bible, v, 55
Blake, 76
Blessedness, 7, 103, 104, 126, 127, 128, 131, 157, 163
Bliss, 7, 25, 50, 103
Boëhme, vi, 11, 158
Bradley, F. H., 77, 78, 84, 132, 133, 134, 158, 161, 162, 163-164, 165, 166
Brahman, 13, 14, 15, 22, 24, 30, 31, 37, 73, 74, 84, 161, 162 163
Buddha, The, 20, 21, 108
Buddhism, 9, 15-25, 29, 87, 107
Bunyan, 63, 95, 134

Causation, identity theory of, 73 n.
Christ, 31, 32
Christianity, 9, 10, 14, 16, 17, 18, 19, 22, 23, 25, 28, 29, 32, 50, 59, 80, 87

Concepts, 33, 38-39, 40, 42, 44, 45, 47, 48, 51, 69, 70, 83
Contradiction, in the Ultimate, 3, 8, 61, 153 ff.
Creation, 12, 52, 53, 72, 73
Croce, 142

Degrees, of reality, 78, 122, 124, 125
Demiurge, 59, 138
Dionysius the Areopagite, 11

Eckhart, 10-11, 15, 20, 24, 25, 157, 158
Ecstasy, 65, 67
Eliot, T. S., 75
Emergent evolution, 81
Epicurus, 56
Eternity, 75, 76, 157
Ethical predicates of God, 100 ff.
Evil, the problem of, 56-57
Evolution and ethics, 101, 105
"Existence," meaning of, 33-34

Faith, and reason, 152
"Finite," meaning of, 42 ff.
Flux, 129, 130
Force, as symbol of God, 98
Fundamentalism, 52

Gandhi, 80
Genesis, v, 53

Hamlet, 95
Hasidic mystics, 12
Heaven, 5, 22
Hedonism, 110
Hegel, 78, 122, 123, 132, 158, 161, 162, 163, 164-166
Hinduism, 9, 12-15, 16, 17, 18, 19, 25, 29, 50, 73, 107
Holy Ghost, 15
Hume, David, 56, 92, 112, 146
Hypnosis, 82

Ibn-al-Arabi, 26
Idealism, absolute, 128, 132-133
Identity, in difference, 163; of opposites, 164, 165, 166
Ideogram, 62, 94
Idolatry, 100
Immanence, God's, 80
Incomprehensibility, of God, 10, 29, 37-40, 41, 42, 49, 65, 93, 154, 166
India, 9, 10, 14, 21, 28, 29, 77, 87, 122
Ineffability, meaning of, 32-40
Infinity, Infinite, The, 4, 5, 7, 59, 62, 70, 73, 74, 76, 123, 157
Intellect, 12, 39, 40, 41, 42, 46, 49, 65, 66, 105, 153
Intuition, 3, 9, 27, 41, 42, 43, 45, 46, 48, 49, 62, 66, 68, 105, 139, 140, 145 151
Inge W. R., 11, 28, 29, 31, 92
Ishwara, 14
Islam, 9, 10, 24-25, 50

Jílí, 25
John of the Cross, 157
Judaism, 9, 10, 11-12, 25, 50

Kabbalists, 12
Kant, v, vi, 87 n., 122, 146-149
Kaufmann, Walter, vii
Keats, 117, 118, 119
Keith, A. B., 19

Leibniz, 113 n.
Life, as symbol of God, 99

Manifestation, 73, 74
Maya, 73, 122, 162
Metaphor, 62-64
Mill, J. S., 108, 110, 111
Mind, as symbol of God, 98
Miracles, 137
Moore, G. E., 108-109, 134
Muller, Max, 18
Music, 5, 16, 120
Mystery, of God, 8, 10, 29, 36-40, 41, 48, 49, 93, 153, 154, 156, 157, 165, 166

Mysticism
   Buddhist, 15-25
   Christian, 10-11
   Hindu, 12-15
   Islamic, 25-26
   Jewish, 11-12

Narada, 6
Naturalism, v, vi, 77, 79, 123, 161
Naturalistic account of values, 102
Newton, v, 72, 112 n., 113 n.
Nirvana, 18, 19, 20, 21, 22, 23, 24, 25, 85
Non-being, 8, 9, 13, 14, 24, 26, 32, 50, 51, 59, 67, 164
Nothing, Nothingness, 8, 10, 11, 12, 15, 20, 24, 26, 27, 28, 29, 30, 32, 33, 65, 67

Object, and subject, 40, 45, 62, 71, 77, 84, 97
Omnipresence, God's, 72, 79, 80, 85
Otto, Rudolph, vii, 15 n., 18, 93, 94, 95

Panpsychism, 81
Pantheism, 80
Parmenides, 122, 133
Pascal, 146, 147
Paul, St., 87
Personality, as symbol of God, 98
Plato, 63, 106, 107, 122, 124, 125, 127, 128, 129, 133
Plotinus, 40, 91
Power, as symbol of God, 98, 99
Proofs, of God's existence, 136-138, 146 ff.

Reality, God as supreme, 121 ff.; and value, 127
Reason, its function in religion, 146, 152, 153
Reincarnation, 25
Relation, of God to the world, 71 ff.
Revelation, 32, 48, 89, 120, 139, 140, 151, 152

Sankara, 14, 15, 25, 30, 163
Sankhya, 18
Scale, of being, 96; of values, 100 ff.
Scepticism, 54, 55-60, 79
Schleiermacher, vii
Scholem, G. G., 11, 12
Self-realization, of God, 96, 97
Shakespeare, 63
Shehadi, F., vii
Shock, poetic, 118, 119
Siva, 50
Smith, Margaret, 26 ff.
Sophocles, 16
Spinoza, 47, 85, 122, 123, 128, 133, 158, 161, 162, 163, 165
Subconscious, 77, 81, 91, 92, 96, 97, 118
Subject and object, 40, 45, 62, 71, 77, 84, 97
Sufi, 25
Symbolic interpretation of theology, 51 ff.

Tauler, 11, 26, 29, 31, 32, 157
Theology, 46, 52
Tillich, Paul, vi
Time, the unreality of, 129
Toynbee, Arnold, 17, 18
Trance, 67

Transcendence, God's, 80
Trinity, The, 8, 37, 40, 45, 47, 140, 154, 158
Truth, as attribute of God, 116 ff.

Unchangeableness, God's, 58, 59
Unknowable, 65
Upanishads, The, 7, 12, 14, 17, 19, 31, 33, 37, 40, 47, 123, 125, 157, 158, 159, 160, 162

Values, scale of, 117; naturalistic theory of, 102
Vedanta, 14, 18, 78, 85, 161
Void, 15, 19, 20, 30, 31, 32, 33, 34, 65, 67, 157, 162, 165

Whitehead, A. N., 3, 8, 81, 159, 160
Wordsworth, 117, 118, 119

Yoga, 18

Zen, 85, 86
Zeno, the Electic, 133, 134
Zimmer, H., 50